Fast Fresh Food

NOTES

All recipes serve four people.

Both metric and imperial measurements are given for the recipes. Use one set of measures only, not a mixture of both.

Ovens should be preheated to the specified temperature. If using a fan-assisted oven, follow the manufacturer's instructions for adjusting the time and temperature. Grills should also be preheated.

This book includes dishes made with nuts and nut derivatives. It is advisable for those with known allergic reactions to nuts and nut derivatives and those who may be potentially vulnerable to these allergies, such as pregnant and nursing mothers, invalids, the elderly, babies and children, to avoid dishes made with nuts and nut oils. It is also prudent to check the labels of preprepared ingredients for the possible inclusion of nut derivatives.

The Department of Health advises that eggs should not be consumed raw. This book contains some dishes made with raw or lightly cooked eggs. It is prudent for more vulnerable people such as pregnant and nursing mothers, invalids, the elderly, babies and young children to avoid uncooked or lightly cooked dishes made with eggs.

Meat and poultry should be cooked thoroughly. To test if poultry is cooked, pierce the flesh through the thickest part with a skewer or fork – the juices should run clear, never pink or red.

Fresh herbs should be used unless otherwise stated. If unavailable, use dried herbs as an alternative but halve the quantities stated.

First published in Great Britain in 2005 by
Hamlyn, a division of Octopus Publishing Group Ltd
2–4 Heron Quays, London E14 4JP

First published in paperback in 2006

ISBN-13: 978-0-600-61582-8
ISBN-10: 0-600-61582-0

A CIP catalogue record for this book is available from the British Library

Printed and bound in China

10 9 8 7 6 5 4 3 2 1

hamlyn

Fast Fresh Food

180 great-tasting recipes in no time

Tonia George, Sara Lewis and Louise Pickford

Contents

Introduction

When we are short on time and energy after a hard day at work, most of us cook the same narrow repertoire of dishes night after night, or even resort to ready meals. Wouldn't it be nice to come home to a different, exciting home-cooked meal every night? Perhaps a *Warm pork and noodle salad*, *Seabass with roasted fennel and salsa verde*, or *Cannellini bean and saffron stew*. And all for just 15 minutes in the kitchen.

This book presents 180 mouth-watering recipes aimed at busy people who appreciate a decent meal. They are accessible and easy to achieve, but most of all varied and interesting. Not only will your palate enjoy this new approach, but your health will also benefit. By avoiding ready meals, you will cut down on fat, salt and additives, and by using a wider range of fresh ingredients you will greatly improve your intake of nutrients.

The recipes
The recipes have been devised so that you need only be in the kitchen for a maximum of 15 minutes. They may require longer in the oven or on the stove, but you will be free to put your feet up with a glass of wine and relax while your meal cooks. Alternatively, you could prepare the meal in the morning before you go out and enjoy the

benefits when you return. There are recipes for many different occasions, featuring cuisines from all over the world. There are sections for soups, starters and snacks, main meals and desserts. The main meals are divided by theme so you can pick a dish you fancy. The chapters are Light and healthy; Pasta, rice and pizza; Oriental; Vegetarian; Fish and seafood; and Meat and poultry. Each recipe makes enough for four people, but if you fancy having a starter as a main course, you can always make double the amount.

The secret of 15-minute feasts

The key to producing delicious meals in little time is careful planning. You need to have a selection of ingredients to hand and they need to be ingredients which are quick and easy to prepare. Some foods by their very nature need to be cooked briefly for best results. Think fresh tuna and swordfish, tender steaks, fresh pasta, prawns, asparagus spears or leafy spinach. All of them take very little time to cook so they are perfect for meals in minutes.

Keeping a well-stocked storecupboard is another secret to success in the kitchen. The following ingredients will allow you to produce interesting meals every day:

- **Starchy staples:** spaghetti, penne, risotto and basmati rice, couscous and noodles.
- **Canned and bottled foods:** beans and lentils, chopped tomatoes, passata, tuna fish, sardines, smoked oysters, artichoke hearts, marinated peppers and olives.
- **Fresh flavourings:** ginger, garlic, chillies and herbs. These can all be chopped and frozen for future use.
- **Other useful ingredients:** curry pastes, soy sauce, Thai fish sauce, dried spices, vinegars, olive oil, sunflower oil and sesame oil.

Time-saving tips

- Even if you have very little time each day for cooking, put aside an hour or two each week for carefully planned shopping so you have the right ingredients for a range of tempting meals.
- If you are really short on time, buy ready-prepared vegetables, ready-diced meat, or fish fillets from a supermarket.
- Make a double quantity of a recipe and freeze half for another meal. Stocks, sauces, stews, casseroles and curries all freeze extremely well.
- Some frozen foods make time-saving sense. Stock the freezer with interesting breads, bags of frozen vegetables, raw or ready-cooked prawns, free-flow minced beef or lamb, ready-made sauces and tubs of good-quality ice cream for an instant dessert.
- Always have some quick-cook vegetables handy. Spinach, courgettes, broccoli, tomatoes and mushrooms will all make a flavoursome meal with pasta, risotto, couscous or noodles.

Introduction 7

Soups, starters and snacks

Fresh tomato and almond soup

The addition of ground almonds not only flavours this delicious soup but helps to thicken it as well. Make it during the summer months when tomatoes are at their juiciest and best. To toast the almonds, dry-fry them in a frying pan over a medium heat, stirring constantly until golden brown.

1 kg (2 lb) vine-ripened tomatoes, roughly chopped

2 garlic cloves, crushed

300 ml (½ pint) vegetable stock

2 tablespoons extra virgin olive oil

1 teaspoon caster sugar

100 g (3½ oz) ground almonds, toasted

salt and pepper

BASIL OIL

150 ml (¼ pint) extra virgin olive oil

15 g (½ oz) basil leaves

Place the roughly chopped tomatoes in a saucepan with the garlic, stock, oil and sugar, and add salt and pepper. Bring to the boil and simmer gently for 15 minutes.

Meanwhile, prepare the basil oil. Purée the oil, basil leaves and a pinch of salt in a blender or food processor until really smooth. Then set aside.

Stir the almonds into the soup, warm it through and then serve in warmed bowls, drizzled with the basil oil.

Beetroot gazpacho

This stunning, deep-pink soup is even better if allowed to infuse and chill for an hour before serving. It makes a perfect no-fuss appetizer for entertaining because you can prepare it in advance and simply serve it when you and your guests are ready to eat.

500 g (1 lb) cooked beetroot in natural juices, drained and chopped
1 small onion, roughly chopped
2 garlic cloves, roughly chopped
2 tomatoes, roughly chopped
2 tablespoons capers, drained
4 baby cornichons, drained and chopped

25 g (1 oz) dried breadcrumbs
600 ml (1 pint) vegetable stock
150 ml (¼ pint) extra virgin olive oil
2 tablespoons white wine vinegar
salt and pepper

TO SERVE
crème fraîche
chopped dill

Put the beetroot, onion, garlic, tomatoes, capers and cornichons into a blender or food processor and blend until smooth. Add the breadcrumbs and pulse, and then gradually blend in the stock, oil and vinegar to form a smooth soup. Season with salt and pepper and serve topped with a spoonful of crème fraîche and some chopped fresh dill and sprinkled with black pepper.

Truffled leek and potato soup

A drizzle of truffle oil will transform this simple soup into something really special. Truffles are prized among all fungi for their intense flavour and aroma – and although the oil is expensive, you need only a little drizzle and the taste is sublime.

3 leeks, trimmed (about 375 g (12 oz) trimmed weight)
50 g (2 oz) butter
1 onion, chopped
1 garlic clove, crushed
300 g (10 oz) potatoes, diced
900 ml (1½ pints) vegetable stock
salt and pepper

TO GARNISH

truffle oil
chopped chives

Slice the leeks, wash to remove dirt, drain well and dry on kitchen paper.

Melt the butter in a saucepan and fry the onion, garlic and leeks over a medium heat for 5 minutes. Add the potatoes, stock, salt and pepper, bring to the boil, cover and simmer gently for 20 minutes.

Purée the soup in a blender or food processor until really smooth, return to the pan, heat through and adjust the seasoning if necessary. Serve the soup drizzled with truffle oil and chopped chives.

Curried vegetable soup

A warming and satisfying dish for those cold winter nights. Ghee is traditionally used in India for shallow frying and is similar to clarified butter. You can often find ghee in cans in larger supermarkets or seek it out in a specialist Indian food store.

40 g (1½ oz) ghee or butter
1 onion, chopped
2 garlic cloves, crushed
2 teaspoons grated fresh root ginger
1 large potato, diced
1 large carrot, diced
2 teaspoons ground coriander
1 teaspoon ground cumin
½ teaspoon garam masala
125 g (4 oz) red lentils
600 ml (1 pint) vegetable stock
600 ml (1 pint) tomato juice
salt and pepper

TO SERVE
raita
naan bread

Melt the ghee or butter in a saucepan and fry the onion, garlic, ginger, potato and carrot for 10 minutes. Stir in the spices and then add the remaining ingredients. Bring to the boil, cover and simmer over a low heat for 20–25 minutes until the lentils and vegetables are cooked.

Season with salt and pepper, then spoon into warmed bowls. Top each bowl with some raita and serve with naan bread.

Japanese miso soup with noodles

This light, healthy soup has a rich, savoury flavour. Miso is made from fermented soy bean paste and is a classic ingredient in Japanese cooking, along with wakame seaweed and mirin. Look out for miso and wakame in health food stores and larger supermarkets, and mirin in larger supermarkets and specialist Asian food stores.

250 g (8 oz) dried udon noodles

150 g (5 oz) firm tofu, diced

25 g (1 oz) dried wakame seaweed

4 spring onions, thinly sliced

1.5 litres (2½ pints) vegetable stock

3 tablespoons miso paste

2 tablespoons dark soy sauce

2 tablespoons mirin (Japanese cooking wine)

Plunge the noodles into a pan of boiling water and cook for 4 minutes, drain well and transfer to warmed soup bowls. Top with the tofu, wakame and spring onions.

Bring the vegetable stock, miso paste, soy sauce and mirin to the boil and simmer gently for 3–4 minutes. Pour into the bowls and serve at once.

Thai chicken and coconut soup

Thai red curry paste adds the essential fiery heat to this soup, while the Kaffir lime leaves – with their unmistakable aroma – add a sharp citrus punch. You should be able to find fresh Kaffir lime leaves in Asian stores and larger supermarkets. The leaves keep well and can be stored in the refrigerator for up to a month or in the freezer for months at a time.

2 tablespoons vegetable oil

1–2 tablespoons Thai red curry paste

750 g (1½ lb) skinless chicken breast
    fillet, diced

8 Kaffir lime leaves

600 ml (1 pint) chicken stock

200 g (7 oz) French beans, trimmed
    and halved

1 red pepper, cored, deseeded and sliced

400 ml (14 fl oz) can coconut milk

1 tablespoon Thai fish sauce

TO GARNISH

Thai or ordinary basil leaves

sliced red chilli

shredded Kaffir lime leaves

Heat the oil in a wok or deep frying pan, add the curry paste and stir-fry for 1 minute until sizzling. Add the chicken and lime leaves and stir for a further 1 minute until they are evenly coated.

Add the chicken stock, bring to the boil, cover and simmer for 15 minutes. Add the remaining ingredients to the pan and simmer gently for a further 2–3 minutes.

Spoon into warmed bowls and serve topped with basil leaves, sliced red chilli and shredded lime leaves.

Chunky chorizo, pasta and bean soup

This substantial winter soup is based on the Italian classic, *pasta e fagioli* – pasta and beans. Chunks of fiery chorizo sausage add a lovely spiciness to the dish. The tiny pasta shapes used for soup are known as pastina; there are hundreds of different varieties to choose from – use any type you like.

4 tablespoons extra virgin olive oil
1 large onion, chopped
50 g (2 oz) chorizo sausage, chopped
4 garlic cloves, crushed
2 tablespoons chopped thyme
1.2 litres (2 pints) passata (puréed tomatoes)
750 ml (1¼ pints) chicken stock
2 x 400 g (13 oz) cans borlotti beans, rinsed
    and drained
200 g (7 oz) small pasta shapes, such as
    conchigliette
3 tablespoons chopped basil
salt and pepper
freshly grated Parmesan cheese, to serve

Heat the oil in a saucepan and fry the onion, chorizo, garlic and thyme for 5 minutes. Add the passata, stock, drained beans, salt and pepper to the pan. Bring to the boil, cover and simmer for 20 minutes.

Stir in the pasta and basil and cook for a further 8–10 minutes until the pasta is tender. Adjust the seasoning if necessary, spoon into warmed bowls and serve topped with grated Parmesan.

Baked goats' cheese pastries

Ready-rolled sheets of frozen puff pastry are really useful for quick, last-minute meals. Always keep a packet in the freezer to use when guests arrive unannounced. Use a goats' cheese with rind for this dish, rather than the smooth, creamy rindless variety.

1 sheet of ready-rolled frozen puff pastry,
   about 25 cm (10 inches) square, thawed
175 g (6 oz) goats' cheese, cut into 4 slices
2 teaspoons clear honey
4 lemon thyme or thyme sprigs
grated rind of ½ lemon
salt and pepper
salad leaves, to garnish

Cut the pastry into 4 12-cm (5-inch) squares and place a round of cheese in the centre of each one. Drizzle the cheese with a little honey and sprinkle over the thyme, lemon rind, salt and pepper.

Carefully transfer the pastries to a preheated baking sheet and cook in a preheated oven, 220°C (425°F), Gas Mark 7, for 10 minutes until the pastry is puffed up and golden and the cheese browned. Garnish with salad leaves and serve hot.

Smoked mackerel and caraway pâté

This deliciously creamy fish pâté makes a lovely pre-dinner snack – spread on crostini or use as a dip for crudités – and can be made ahead of time – simply cover and chill it until it is required. One large smoked mackerel fillet will give you the required skinned weight.

1 teaspoon caraway seeds
200 g (3½ oz) skinned smoked mackerel fillet
175 g (3 oz) cream cheese
1 tablespoon lemon juice
4 tablespoons crème fraîche
2 tablespoons creamed horseradish sauce
1 tablespoon chopped chives
salt and pepper
toasted rye bread, to serve

Dry-fry the caraway seeds in a small pan for 1–2 minutes until they start to brown and release their aroma. Cool slightly and then grind coarsely, using a pestle and mortar or a spice grinder.

Place the mackerel, cream cheese, lemon juice, crème fraîche, ground caraway seeds, horseradish and chives in a blender or food processor and blend until smooth. Season with salt and pepper, blend again and transfer to a serving bowl. Chill until required, then serve with toasted rye bread.

Glazed spiced nuts

These deliciously moreish honey-glazed nuts make a lovely snack to serve with pre-dinner drinks. Their sweet, smoky, peppery flavour goes particularly well with a chilled, fruity sherry.

25 g (1 oz) butter
3 tablespoons clear honey
1 teaspoon salt
$\frac{1}{2}$ teaspoon smoked paprika
pinch of chilli powder
2 tablespoons water
250 g (8 oz) cashew nuts

Melt the butter in a frying pan and add the honey, salt, spices and measured water. Bring to the boil and stir in the nuts. Cook, stirring, over a medium heat for 4–5 minutes until the nuts are glazed and lightly golden.

Pour them on to a baking sheet lined with nonstick baking paper and spread out the nuts with a wooden spoon. Cool, tap gently if necessary to separate them once more, and serve with drinks.

Pan-fried haloumi with lemon and paprika oil

Haloumi is a semi-hard ewes' milk cheese from Cyprus. It is often flavoured with chopped mint and has a wonderfully salty, sharp flavour and a delicious springy, chewy texture. It is perfectly suited to frying because it retains its shape – eat it as soon as it is cooked, while the outside is crisp and the inside is gooey and meltingly soft.

6 tablespoons extra virgin olive oil
4 tablespoons lemon juice
½ teaspoon smoked paprika
250 g (8 oz) haloumi, cut into chunks
salt and pepper

Combine the oil, lemon juice and paprika in a small bowl and season the mixture with salt and pepper.

Heat a heavy-based frying pan until hot, then add the haloumi and toss over a medium heat until golden and starting to soften. Transfer immediately to a plate, drizzle over the paprika oil and serve with tooth picks to spike the haloumi.

Fresh ricotta with herb oil and radishes

Ricotta served with aromatic herbs and a drizzle of olive oil makes a simple yet sophisticated starter. Look out for ricotta sold in a large mound at the delicatessen section of larger supermarkets; such cheese has a creamier taste and richer flavour than the pre-packed varieties.

375 g (12 oz) fresh ricotta

50 ml (2 fl oz) extra virgin olive oil

1 tablespoon chopped herbs, such as
    basil, chives, mint and parsley

1 bunch of radishes, washed and
    trimmed

salt and pepper

crusty bread, to serve

Cut the ricotta into thin wedges and arrange them on a plate. Combine the oil, herbs, salt and pepper and drizzle over the ricotta. Arrange the radishes around the edge of the plate and serve with crusty bread.

Garlic toasts with creamed avocado

A chunky and satisfying snack that can be served as a starter, with pre-dinner drinks, or at any other time of day when hunger pangs strike. To ensure the avocado is at its best for eating, gently press at the narrow end of the fruit – it should give just a little.

3 tablespoons extra virgin olive oil, plus
   extra to drizzle
1 large garlic clove, crushed
6 thick slices of French bread
1 ripe avocado
1 red chilli, deseeded and finely chopped
1 tablespoon lime juice
salt and pepper
coriander leaves, to garnish

Mix the oil and garlic together and brush all over the bread slices. Place on a baking sheet and cook in a preheated oven, 220°C (425°F), Gas Mark 7, for 6–8 minutes until lightly golden.

Meanwhile, cut the avocado in half, discard the stone and scoop the flesh into a bowl. Mash in the chilli, lime juice, salt and pepper until fairly smooth. Spread over the toasts and serve at once, garnished with coriander leaves and a drizzle of oil.

Fennel and marinated anchovy crostini

These crisp, irresistible toasts are often served as part of an Italian antipasti selection. In this version, the flavours of the zesty, garlicky fennel marry perfectly with the salty anchovies to create a sensational snack or starter. Just make sure you bake plenty of them.

12 slices of French bread
1 fennel bulb, trimmed
1 small garlic clove, crushed
2 tablespoons chopped parsley
6 tablespoons extra virgin olive oil
2 tablespoons lemon juice
24 marinated anchovy fillets, drained
salt and pepper

Arrange the bread slices on a baking sheet and cook in a preheated oven, 220°C (425°F), Gas Mark 7, for 8–10 minutes until crisp and golden, turning half way through. Transfer to a platter.

Remove the outer layer of fennel leaves and discard. Cut the bulb in half lengthways and then cut crossways into wafer-thin slices – you will need about 100 g (3½ oz) of trimmed fennel. Place in a bowl with the garlic and parsley. Add the oil and lemon juice, salt and pepper and toss together until well coated.

Spoon the fennel mixture on to the crostini and top each with 2 marinated anchovy fillets. Drizzle over any remaining dressing from the bowl.

Soups, starters and snacks

Sage and goats' cheese frittata

A frittata is a flat Italian omelette, usually a combination of eggs, sautéed vegetables, herbs and sometimes topped with a little cheese. It makes a perfect light lunch for 2 or a starter for 4 people, and can also be served as a quick savoury snack.

25 g (1 oz) butter
18 large sage leaves
50 g (2 oz) soft goats' cheese, crumbled
2 tablespoons crème fraîche
4 eggs
salt and pepper
crusty bread, to serve

Melt the butter in a nonstick frying pan, add the sage leaves and fry over a low heat for 1–2 minutes until the leaves are crisp and golden and the butter a lovely nutty brown colour. Take out 6 of the leaves and put aside. Pour the rest into a bowl. Beat the goats' cheese and crème fraîche together until combined.

Beat the eggs in a bowl, season with salt and pepper, then stir in the sage butter. Reheat the frying pan (adding a little extra butter if necessary), pour in the egg mixture and dot over spoonfuls of the goats' cheese mixture.

Cook over a medium heat for 4–5 minutes until the bottom is set, then transfer to a preheated hot grill to lightly brown the top. Garnish with the extra sage leaves. Cool slightly, gently slip the frittata on to a plate and serve with crusty bread.

Smoked chicken and avocado salad

Because smoked chicken is hot-smoked, it is already cooked and ready to eat. Take advantage of such tasty, cooked ingredients to throw together salads in minutes. If you are especially short of time, you can buy ready-made croûtons but it is fairly simple to make your own.

6 tablespoons extra virgin olive oil

4 slices of day-old bread, cut into 1-cm
   ($\frac{1}{2}$-inch) dice

500 g (1 lb) smoked chicken breast slices

3 Little Gem or baby Cos lettuce hearts

1 large ripe avocado, peeled, stoned and diced

25 g (1 oz) freshly grated Parmesan cheese

DRESSING

125 ml (4 fl oz) extra virgin olive oil

2 tablespoons tarragon vinegar

1 tablespoon wholegrain mustard

1 tablespoon chopped tarragon

1 teaspoon caster sugar

salt and pepper

To make the croûtons, heat the oil in a frying pan and fry the bread cubes, stirring constantly, for 5–6 minutes until golden on all sides. Drain on kitchen paper.

Cut the chicken breast slices into bite-size pieces and place in a large bowl. Add the lettuce leaves to the chicken with the avocado, croûtons and Parmesan.

Whisk the dressing ingredients together and season with salt and pepper. Pour it over the salad and toss well until it is evenly coated. Serve at once.

Pear, radicchio and pecorino salad

Pecorino is a hard, grainy Italian cheese made from ewes' milk. It has a sweet, nutty, salty flavour and provides a perfect contrast to the slices of sweet, juicy pear and bitter radicchio leaves. This cheese is available in most supermarkets, but Parmesan can be used as an alternative.

6 tablespoons extra virgin olive oil

4 slices of day-old bread, cut into 1-cm
   ($\frac{1}{2}$-inch) dice

2 radicchio heads

2 firm ripe pears

100 g (3$\frac{1}{2}$ oz) Pecorino cheese, diced

a few mint leaves, torn

DRESSING

4 tablespoons hazelnut oil

2 tablespoons extra virgin olive oil

1 tablespoon raspberry vinegar

a pinch of caster sugar

salt and pepper

To make the croûtons, heat the oil in a frying pan and fry the bread cubes, stirring constantly, for 5–6 minutes until golden on all sides. Drain on kitchen paper.

Separate the radicchio leaves, tear into bite-size pieces and place in a large bowl. Peel, core and dice the pears and add to the lettuce with the Pecorino, croûtons and mint leaves.

Place all the dressing ingredients in a screw-top jar and shake until they are well combined. Drizzle over the salad, toss to coat the leaves and serve at once.

Salad of spinach, Gorgonzola and honeyed walnuts

Gorgonzola has a strong, piquant taste and wonderfully creamy texture. If you prefer a milder flavour, use a less-robust blue cheese such as dolcelatte instead. The sweetness of the honey brings out the taste of the toasted walnuts and salty cheese perfectly.

1 tablespoon clear honey
125 g (4 oz) walnut halves
250 g (8 oz) French beans,
    trimmed
200 g (7 oz) baby spinach leaves
150 g (5 oz) Gorgonzola,
    crumbled

DRESSING
4 tablespoons walnut oil
2 tablespoons extra virgin olive oil
1–2 tablespoons sherry vinegar
salt and pepper

Heat the honey in a small frying pan, add the walnuts and stir-fry over a medium heat for 2–3 minutes until the nuts are glazed. Tip them on to a plate and leave to cool.

Meanwhile, blanch the beans in lightly salted boiling water for 3 minutes, drain, refresh under cold water and shake dry. Place in a large bowl with the spinach leaves.

Whisk the dressing ingredients together and season with salt and pepper. Pour over the salad and toss well to coat the leaves. Arrange the salad in bowls, scatter over the Gorgonzola and honeyed walnuts and serve at once.

Fig, mozzarella and prosciutto salad

Verjuice, made from unripe grapes, has a strong, acidic flavour and is used in cooking as an alternative to lemon juice or vinegar. It gives the dressing a lovely flavour, but if you cannot find it, use a good quality white wine vinegar sweetened with a pinch of sugar instead.

8–12 ripe black figs

250 g (8 oz) buffalo mozzarella

8 slices of prosciutto

a few basil leaves

DRESSING

3 tablespoons extra virgin olive oil

1 tablespoon verjuice

salt and pepper

Cut the figs into quarters, tear the mozzarella and prosciutto into bite-size pieces and arrange on a large platter with the basil leaves.

Whisk together the olive oil, verjuice, salt and pepper. Drizzle the dressing over the salad and serve it at once.

Tomato, tapenade and feta tart

This tasty and colourful tart makes a perfect appetizer or snack. Basil-infused oil is a simple way of adding extra flavour to the tart and is available in most supermarkets. Alternatively, you can make your own (see page 9) or simply scatter over a handful of fresh basil leaves just before serving and drizzle with good-quality extra virgin olive oil.

1 sheet of ready-rolled frozen puff pastry,
    about 25 cm (10 inches) square, thawed
2 tablespoons olive tapenade
250 g (8 oz) cherry tomatoes, halved
100 g (3½ oz) feta cheese, diced
2 tablespoons freshly grated Parmesan cheese
2 tablespoons basil oil
black pepper
green salad, to serve

Trim the edges of the pastry square then use the blade of a sharp knife to gently tap the edges – this will help the pastry rise. Prick all over the pastry with a fork and place it on a baking sheet.

Spread the pastry with the tapenade, leaving a 1 cm (½ inch) border. Scatter over the tomatoes, feta and Parmesan. Season with pepper and place the baking sheet on a second preheated baking sheet. Cook in a preheated oven, 220°C (425°F), Gas Mark 7, for 15–18 minutes until golden.

Drizzle the basil oil over the tart and serve with green salad.

Tuna tartare

Because the tuna is marinated rather than cooked, you need to use really good-quality fish for this recipe; if you can, buy sushi-quality tuna loin. Crispy wontons make perfect dippers for scooping up the spicy fish. You can buy the paper-thin fresh wonton wrappers from larger supermarkets and specialist Oriental food stores.

250 g (8 oz) tuna loin
1 tablespoon chopped fresh coriander
1 red bird's eye chilli, deseeded and finely chopped
1 tablespoon light soy sauce
2 teaspoons sesame oil
8–12 wonton wrappers
Szechuan pepper
sunflower oil, for shallow frying

Cut the tuna into slices and then into small dice, removing any gristle or membrane as you go. Use a large knife to chop the tuna until it is very finely diced and even appears a little mushy.

Place in a bowl and stir in the coriander, chilli, soy sauce, sesame oil and some Szechuan pepper. Chill until required.

Cut the wontons diagonally in half. Heat 1 cm (½ inch) of sunflower oil in a frying pan and shallow fry the wontons for 30 seconds until crisp and golden. Drain on kitchen paper. Serve the tuna in mounds with the crispy wontons.

Smoked salmon Thai rolls

Impress friends and family with these pretty parcels as a sophisticated starter or snack with pre-dinner drinks. The sweet, salty, sharp flavours of the Thai dressing make an unusual, yet utterly delicious, flavouring for the smoked salmon. Thai basil leaves are usually available in Asian stores and have a wonderful aniseed flavour, but you can use ordinary sweet basil instead.

12 slices of smoked salmon

1 cucumber, peeled, deseeded and cut
into matchsticks

1 long red chilli, deseeded and thinly sliced

a handful each of coriander, mint and
Thai basil leaves

DRESSING

2 tablespoons sweet chilli sauce

2 tablespoons clear honey

2 tablespoons lime juice

1 tablespoon Thai fish sauce

Separate the smoked salmon slices and lay them flat on a work surface. Divide the cucumber, chilli and herbs between the smoked salmon slices, placing them in a mound on each slice.

Combine the dressing ingredients and drizzle over the filling. Roll up the salmon slices to enclose the filling and serve on a large platter.

Light and healthy

Griddled tuna and warm bean salad

Tuna is best cooked rare so that the middle of the steak is still pink and juicy. You can cook it for a little longer if you prefer but be careful not to overcook because it will become tough and dry.

4 tuna steaks, about 200 g (7 oz) each
7 tablespoons extra virgin olive oil, plus extra
    to serve
2 garlic cloves, crushed
2 teaspoons chopped rosemary
pinch of dried red chilli flakes
2 x 400 g (13 oz) cans cannellini beans, rinsed
    and drained
4 plum tomatoes, deseeded and diced
½ red onion, finely chopped
1½ tablespoons red wine vinegar
2 tablespoons chopped parsley
salt and pepper
parsley leaves, to garnish

Brush the tuna steaks with a little of the oil, and season with salt and pepper. Heat 4 tablespoons of the remaining oil in a frying pan and gently fry the garlic, rosemary and chilli flakes for 1–2 minutes until softened.

Add the beans, tomatoes and red onion, and season with salt and pepper. Cook gently for 5 minutes until heated through. Remove the pan from the heat and stir in the remaining oil, the vinegar and parsley.

Meanwhile, sear the tuna steaks in a preheated ridged grill pan for 45 seconds on each side or longer for a less pink centre. Remove from the pan, wrap loosely in foil and leave to rest.

Spoon the beans on to individual plates, then slice the tuna steaks and place them on top with any juices. Serve at once, drizzled with a little extra oil.

Halibut parcels with saffron, tomatoes and orange

These meaty halibut fillets are cooked in foil parcels to trap all the wonderful flavours and juices as the fish cooks. Be careful when opening the parcels because the escaping steam will be hot.

4 tablespoons orange juice
pinch of saffron threads
4 halibut fillets, about 200 g
   (7 oz) each
2 tablespoons extra virgin olive oil
3 ripe tomatoes, diced

2 garlic cloves, finely chopped
4 tablespoons dry sherry
4 basil sprigs
grated rind of $\frac{1}{2}$ orange
salt and pepper
mashed potato, to serve

Put the orange juice and saffron threads in a bowl and set aside. Take a large rectangle of foil and place a halibut fillet in the middle. Pull the edges of the foil up around the fish to form a 'bowl'. Repeat to make 4.

Divide the oil, tomatoes, garlic, sherry, basil, orange rind and saffron-infused orange juice between the parcels and season generously with salt and pepper. Bring the edges of the foil up to meet and fold them over to make sealed parcels.

Transfer the parcels to a baking sheet and bake in a preheated oven, 190°C (375°F), Gas Mark 5, for 10 minutes. Remove from the oven and leave to rest for 5 minutes. Carefully tear open the parcels and tip the contents on to warmed plates. Serve with mashed potato.

Asian grilled chicken in pittas

This Asian-style pitta sandwich makes a great lunchtime snack. Coriander roots are often used in Thai dishes to add a lovely fragrant aroma. Buy the coriander in a bunch rather than in a packet, when the roots will have been removed.

8 coriander roots, roughly chopped

$1/4$ teaspoon freshly ground black peppercorns

2 large garlic cloves, roughly chopped

1 tablespoon Thai fish sauce

1 tablespoon light soy sauce

2 teaspoons caster sugar

500 g (1 lb) skinless chicken breast fillet, diced

TO SERVE

4 pitta breads

salad leaves

basil, mint and coriander leaves

sweet chilli sauce

Use a pestle and mortar or spice grinder to grind the coriander, pepper and garlic to a paste. Stir in the fish sauce, soy sauce and sugar. Toss with the chicken, then thread the chicken on to 8 metal skewers and marinate it for at least 1 hour.

Place the kebabs on a grill rack and cook under a preheated hot grill for 3–4 minutes each side until browned and cooked through. Cover with foil and rest for 5 minutes.

Lightly toast the pittas and stuff each one with some salad leaves and herbs. Slip the chicken from the skewers into the pittas and serve topped with sweet chilli sauce.

Warm pasta salad

Malloreddus is a rice-shaped pasta available from larger supermarkets and specialist Italian food stores. It is often used in soups, but here it is combined with peas, marinated artichoke hearts and fresh herbs to make a deliciously fresh warm salad.

250 g (8 oz) malloreddus or orzo pasta
250 g (8 oz) frozen peas, thawed
6 tablespoons extra virgin olive oil
6 spring onions, trimmed and roughly chopped
2 garlic cloves, crushed
8 marinated artichoke hearts, thickly sliced
4 tablespoons chopped mint
rind and juice of ½ lemon
salt and pepper
lemon rind, to garnish

Cook the malloreddus in a saucepan of lightly salted boiling water for about 6 minutes, add the peas and cook for a further 2–3 minutes until the peas and pasta are cooked. Drain well.

Meanwhile, heat 2 tablespoons of the oil in a frying pan and stir-fry the spring onions and garlic for 1–2 minutes until softened. Stir in the malloreddus with the artichokes, mint and remaining oil.

Toss well, season with salt and pepper, then leave to rest for 10 minutes. Stir in the lemon juice and serve the salad warm, garnished with lemon rind.

Soba noodle salad with sesame dressing

Soba noodles are made from buckwheat and are probably the best-known of all the Japanese noodles. They are darker than egg noodles and have a distinctive flavour and texture. There is also a dark green variety, *chasoba*, which is made with buckwheat and green tea. You can find both types in large supermarkets and specialist food stores.

400 g (13 oz) dried soba noodles

250 g (8 oz) thin asparagus spears, trimmed

6 spring onions, trimmed and thinly sliced

50 g (2 oz) baby spinach leaves

DRESSING

75 g (3 oz) sesame seeds

3 tablespoons caster sugar

3 tablespoons dark soy sauce

125 ml (4 fl oz) water

Cook the noodles in a saucepan of lightly salted boiling water for 4 minutes. Drain, refresh under cold water and drain again. Steam the asparagus spears for 2 minutes until tender, drain, refresh under cold water and pat dry.

To make the dressing, grind the sesame seeds to a fine powder, using a spice or coffee grinder; transfer this to a bowl and blend in the remaining ingredients.

Arrange the noodles, asparagus spears, spring onions and spinach leaves in individual bowls, pour over the dressing and serve at once.

Spinach and rice soup

This delicious, hearty soup contains poached eggs, making it a nutritious meal in itself. Poaching the eggs in the soup is a great way to save time – and saves on the washing up, too.

2 tablespoons extra virgin olive oil,
    plus extra to serve
1 onion, finely chopped
2 garlic cloves, finely chopped
300 g (10 oz) baby spinach leaves
900 ml (1 ½ pints) vegetable stock
175 g (6 oz) arborio rice
4 eggs
salt and pepper
freshly grated Parmesan cheese,
    to serve (optional)

Heat the oil in a saucepan and gently fry the onion and garlic for 5 minutes until they have softened. Roughly shred the spinach leaves, add to the pan and cook, stirring, until the spinach has wilted.

Add the stock and rice and season with salt and pepper. Bring the soup to the boil, cover and simmer gently for 15 minutes until the rice is cooked.

Carefully break the eggs into the soup so that they sit on the surface; replace the lid and cook gently for a further 5–6 minutes until the eggs are poached. Serve the soup in warmed bowls drizzled with a little extra oil and some grated Parmesan, if you like.

Light and healthy

Spiced swordfish with fennel and mint salad

Swordfish is a wonderfully meaty fish, which requires only a short cooking time; if you overcook this type of fish it can become dry and tough. It's also a good idea to let your fish rest, like meat, before eating to maximize its moistness and tenderness.

2 teaspoons crushed coriander seeds

4 swordfish steaks, about 200 g (7 oz) each

4–6 tablespoons extra virgin olive oil

1 large fennel bulb, trimmed

1 garlic clove, thinly sliced

2 tablespoons baby capers in salt, rinsed

handful of mint leaves

1–2 tablespoons lemon juice

salt and pepper

rocket leaves, to serve

Combine the coriander seeds with some salt and pepper. Brush the swordfish fillets with a little of the oil and rub over the spice mix. Set aside until ready to cook.

Discard the tough outer layer of fennel, cut the bulb in half lengthways and then crossways, into wafer-thin slices. Place in a bowl with the garlic, capers, mint leaves, remaining oil and lemon juice. Season with salt and pepper.

Cook the swordfish steaks in a preheated ridged grill pan for 1½ minutes on each side, then wrap in foil and leave to rest for 5 minutes. Serve the swordfish and any juices with the fennel salad and rocket.

Smoked trout and cashew salad

This salad offers a lovely combination of flavours and colours – rich smoky trout, sweet mango, fresh aromatic herbs and spicy hot chillies. This recipe will serve 4 as light snack or starter, or 2 as a main course. Bird's eye chillies are the tiny, fiery chillies used in Thai cooking, so use with caution.

500 g (1 lb) smoked trout fillets, skinned
   and flaked
1 ripe mango, peeled, stoned and sliced
4 spring onions, trimmed and sliced
1–2 red bird's eye chillies, deseeded and sliced
handful of mint leaves
handful of coriander leaves
4 tablespoons roasted cashew nuts,
   roughly chopped

DRESSING

2 tablespoons caster sugar
2 tablespoons lime juice
2 tablespoons Thai fish sauce
2 tablespoons water
1 teaspoon grated fresh root ginger
1 teaspoon sesame oil

Start by making the dressing. Warm together the sugar, lime juice, fish sauce, water and ginger until the sugar has dissolved. Remove from the heat, cool and stir in the sesame oil.

Place the trout in a large bowl. Add the mango, spring onions, chilli and herbs. Pour over the dressing and sprinkle with the cashews.

Greek salad, Cyprus style

A delicious variation on the classic Greek salad, this version uses melting slices of fried haloumi cheese (from Cyprus) in place of the traditional feta. The combination of fresh, crunchy salad vegetables, zesty lemon juice and salty cheese is divine and is perfect for a light lunch or supper.

6 ripe tomatoes, roughly chopped
1 cucumber, halved and thickly sliced
1 red onion, thinly sliced
125 g (4 oz) kalamata olives
extra virgin olive oil, for drizzling
lemon juice, for drizzling
1 teaspoon dried oregano
250 g (8 oz) haloumi cheese
salt and pepper

Combine the tomatoes, cucumber, onion and olives in a large bowl, and drizzle with olive oil and lemon juice to taste. Season with oregano, salt and pepper and divide between 4 serving bowls.

Cut the haloumi into 8 slices. Heat a little oil in a heavy-based frying pan and cook the haloumi for 1 minute on each side until it is browned and melting. Top the salads with the haloumi and serve immediately, drizzled with a little extra oil.

Oven-roasted pork fillet

Pork fillet is a particularly lean cut of meat, making it a healthy option. However, you could use pork chops instead. Here, it is served with a parsley and almond pesto.

2 pork tenderloin fillets, about 400 g (13 oz) each
6 tablespoons extra virgin olive oil
50 g (2 oz) blanched almonds
1 garlic clove, crushed
1 bunch of flat leaf parsley
2 tablespoons freshly grated Parmesan cheese
salt and pepper

TO SERVE
boiled new potatoes
green salad

Trim off any gristle from the pork fillets, cut them in half crossways, and season with salt and pepper. Heat 1 tablespoon of the oil in a frying pan and fry the meat for 2–3 minutes until browned on all sides. Transfer to a roasting dish and cook in a preheated oven, 190°C (375°F), Gas Mark 5, for 15 minutes, until cooked through. Remove from the oven, wrap in foil and leave to rest for 5 minutes.

Meanwhile, dry-fry the almonds in a clean frying pan, stirring until browned; allow to cool slightly. Place in a food processor with the garlic, parsley, remaining oil and salt and pepper. Blend to form a fairly smooth paste. Stir in the Parmesan and adjust the seasoning if necessary.

Slice the pork, arrange it on plates with any pan juices and serve it with boiled new potatoes and salad drizzled with spoonfuls of the pesto.

Miso-grilled salmon kebabs with cucumber salad

There are several different varieties of miso paste, all with their own distinct flavour. Choose red or brown miso for this dish, rather than the milder, sweeter white paste. Making kebabs is a quick and easy way to serve salmon, but you can simply grill whole salmon fillets. Whole fillets should be grilled for an extra 2 minutes each side.

2 tablespoons dark soy sauce
2 tablespoons sake or dry sherry
2 tablespoons clear honey
2 tablespoons miso paste
4 skinless salmon fillets, about
    200 g (7 oz) each, cut into cubes
2 small cucumbers, deseeded
    and sliced

1 red bird's eye chilli, deseeded
    and finely chopped
plain boiled rice, to serve

DRESSING

3 tablespoons rice wine vinegar
3 tablespoons caster sugar
3 tablespoons water
$\frac{1}{2}$ teaspoon salt

Stir the soy sauce, sake or sherry, honey and miso together until smooth and pour into a shallow dish. Add the salmon fillets and marinate for as long as possible, turning occasionally in the marinade.

Meanwhile, combine the dressing ingredients in a small saucepan and heat gently to dissolve the sugar, then set aside to cool. Mix in the cucumber and chilli.

Thread the cubes of salmon on to 4 skewers. Cook under a preheated hot grill for 3–4 minutes on each side until charred and cooked through. Serve with the cucumber salad and some boiled rice.

Poached chicken with vegetable broth

For the best results, it is worth buying a good-quality fresh chicken stock for this dish. Fresh stocks are available in the chiller section of large supermarkets as well as at good butchers.

2 tablespoons extra virgin olive oil

1 onion, finely chopped

1 garlic clove, finely chopped

150 ml (¼ pint) dry white wine

600 ml (1 pint) fresh chicken stock

4 large skinless chicken breast fillets, about
   200 g (7 oz) each

200 g (7 oz) frozen broad beans, thawed

200 g (7 oz) frozen peas, thawed

4 tablespoons chopped herbs, such as chives,
   mint, oregano and parsley

salt and pepper

Heat the oil in a frying pan and gently fry the onion and garlic for 5 minutes. Add the wine and boil to reduce by half and then add the stock. Add the chicken fillets, bring to a gentle simmer, cover and cook for 8 minutes. Remove the chicken from the pan, wrap it in foil and keep it warm.

Add the beans and peas to the stock and cook for 2–3 minutes until tender, then add the herbs and season with salt and pepper. Divide the vegetables and poaching liquid between 4 large soup plates. Slice the chicken and arrange in the plates. Serve immediately.

Pan-fried mullet with orange and olive salad

This pretty, refreshing dish is perfect for entertaining and would make an ideal summer lunch. The lightly spiced salad combination of oranges, cinnamon and olives gives this dish a distinctive North African flavour. When cooking small fish fillets, always fry them skin side down first to prevent the fish from curling up in the pan. You could use other fish fillets such as bream or trout.

3 large oranges
50 g (2 oz) raisins
¼ teaspoon ground cinnamon
5 tablespoons extra virgin olive oil,
    plus extra to serve
1 large handful of flat leaf parsley
100 g (3½ oz) green olives
4 red mullet fillets, about 150 g (5 oz)
    each
salt and pepper

Squeeze the juice of 1 orange into a bowl and add the raisins, cinnamon and 4 tablespoons of olive oil. Set aside to soak for 10 minutes.

Peel and segment the remaining oranges (cut the segments in half if large) and place in a large bowl. Pick the leaves from the parsley and add to the oranges with the olives. Season with salt and pepper.

Brush the mullet fillets with the remaining oil and season with salt and pepper on both sides. Heat a heavy-based frying pan and cook the fillets skin side down for 2 minutes, turn over and cook for a further 2 minutes. Transfer to serving plates and rest briefly.

Add the orange juice dressing to the orange and olive salad, toss well and serve with the pan-fried mullet. Drizzle with a little extra oil, if you like.

Healthy spiced chips with smoky tomato salsa

This is a great snack for anyone who loves chips, but avoids them because of their high fat content. Here, the potato wedges are coated with spices and egg white and then baked, rather than fried, to give a wonderfully crisp exterior but a soft fluffy centre. For the best results, use a multipurpose variety of potato, such as Maris Piper.

8 potatoes, about 150 g
(5 oz) each
2 egg whites
1 teaspoon ground paprika
pinch of cayenne pepper
salt and pepper
olive oil spray, for greasing

SMOKY TOMATO SALSA
4 ripe tomatoes
2 garlic cloves
1 red onion, cut into wedges
4 tablespoons extra virgin olive oil
1 tablespoon lime juice
2 tablespoons chopped fresh coriander

Cut the potatoes into chunky wedges and place in a bowl. Lightly whisk the egg whites until frothy and stir into the potatoes wedges so they are evenly coated. Add the spices and plenty of salt and pepper and toss again to lightly coat the wedges with seasoning.

Arrange the wedges in a single layer on a baking sheet lined with nonstick baking paper and sprayed with olive oil. Cook them in a preheated oven, 230°C (450°F), Gas Mark 8, for about 45 minutes, turning a couple of times until roasted and golden.

To make the salsa, cook the tomatoes under a preheated hot grill, turning, for 1–2 minutes until the skin chars and blisters. Skewer the garlic cloves and onion wedges on a long metal skewer and grill for 3–4 minutes on each side until they are charred and softened.

Peel, deseed and finely chop the tomatoes, peel and crush the garlic and finely chop the onion. Place in a bowl and add the remaining ingredients, salt and pepper, and serve with the potato wedges.

Anchovy and sprouting broccoli
bruschetta

Sweet sprouting broccoli florets, tossed in a tangy anchovy dressing, make a delicious topping for crispy bruschetta. Serve as a tempting light meal or a hearty snack.

4 tablespoons extra virgin olive oil
pinch of dried red chilli flakes
pared rind of 1 lemon
2 garlic cloves, crushed
4 anchovy fillets in oil, drained and chopped
625 g (1¼ lb) sprouting broccoli, cut into pieces
1 tablespoon lemon juice
4 slices of sourdough bread
salt and pepper
Parmesan shavings, to garnish

Heat the oil in a small saucepan and gently fry the chilli, lemon rind, garlic and anchovy for 1–2 minutes until softened but not browned. The anchovy should start to melt into the oil; keep warm.

Cook the broccoli in a saucepan of lightly salted boiling water for 3 minutes until just tender. Drain really well and return to the pan. Add the anchovy mixture, lemon juice and some pepper and toss until the broccoli is evenly coated.

Meanwhile, toast the bread on both sides. Arrange it on plates and top with the broccoli mixture. Serve garnished with Parmesan shavings.

Marsala duck salad with roasted peaches

Marsala is a Sicilian fortified wine with an intense, sweet herb flavour. It is available from supermarkets and wine shops, but you could use port as a substitute. To remove the duck skin, hold the breast fillet at one end and pull the skin away from the meat. You may need to use a sharp knife to help ease the skin away from the flesh.

4 peaches, stoned and quartered

1 tablespoon caster sugar

$\frac{1}{2}$ teaspoon ground cinnamon

4 duck breast fillets, about 250 g (8 oz) each, skinned

4 tablespoons extra virgin olive oil

50 ml (2 fl oz) Marsala

2 tablespoons balsamic vinegar

salt and pepper

salad leaves, to serve

Place the peach quarters, cut side up, in a roasting tin. Combine the sugar and cinnamon, sprinkle it evenly over the peaches and cook them in a preheated oven, 220°C (425°F), Gas Mark 7, for 15 minutes or until softened but not collapsed.

Meanwhile, season the duck breasts with salt and pepper. Heat 1 tablespoon of the oil in a frying pan and fry the duck for 3–4 minutes on each side. Remove from the pan, wrap loosely in foil and rest for 5 minutes.

Combine the Marsala and vinegar and add to the pan, boil until reduced by half and then strain into a bowl. Whisk in the remaining oil and any juices from the duck, and season with salt and pepper.

Arrange the peach quarters on plates, thinly slice the duck and arrange it on the plates with some salad leaves. Pour over the dressing and serve at once.

Roasted cherry tomato and ricotta pasta

This piquant, herb-scented dish can be made with just about any shape or variety of pasta you like. Always check the packet for cooking instructions because cooking times will vary.

500 g (1 lb) cherry tomatoes, halved
4 tablespoons extra virgin olive oil
2 teaspoons chopped thyme
4 garlic cloves, sliced
pinch of dried red chilli flakes
400 g (13 oz) dried pasta
1 bunch of basil leaves, torn
125 g (4 oz) ricotta, crumbled
salt and pepper

Place the tomatoes in a roasting tin with the oil, thyme, garlic and chilli, and season with salt and pepper. Cook in a preheated oven, 200°C (400°F), Gas Mark 6, for 15–20 minutes, until the tomatoes have softened and released their juices.

Meanwhile, cook the pasta in a saucepan of lightly salted boiling water for 10–12 minutes or according to packet instructions. Drain and return to the pan.

Stir the tomatoes with their pan juices and most of the basil leaves into the cooked pasta and toss gently until combined. Season with salt and pepper and spoon into bowls. Chop the remaining basil, mix into the ricotta, season with salt and pepper and spoon into a small dish for guests to spoon on to the pasta.

Spaghetti with Thai flavours

East meets West in this spicy, aromatic dish – Italian pasta is tossed with hot and pungent Asian ingredients to create a totally delicious combination. Serve as a starter or light supper dish with a crunchy green salad on the side.

250 g (8 oz) dried spaghetti

4 tablespoons extra virgin olive oil

2 teaspoons sesame oil

2 garlic cloves, sliced

$\frac{1}{2}$ teaspoon grated fresh root ginger

2 red bird's eye chillies, deseeded and finely chopped

grated rind and juice of 2 limes

1 bunch of fresh coriander, chopped

handful of Thai or ordinary basil leaves

salt and pepper

Cook the pasta in a large saucepan of lightly salted boiling water for 10–12 minutes or according to packet instructions. Reserve 4 tablespoons of the cooking liquid, then drain the pasta and return it to the pan.

Meanwhile, heat the two oils together in a frying pan, add the garlic, ginger, chillies and lime rind and fry gently for about 30 seconds, until the garlic starts to release its aroma. Whisk in the reserved pasta water and bring to the boil.

Stir into the pasta with the herbs and lime juice and toss over the heat for a few seconds until heated through. Season with salt and pepper and serve immediately.

Peppered lamb salad with minted yogurt dressing

Succulent slices of lamb with a pepper crust make a delicious topping for this simple watercress and beetroot salad. The meat used in this dish comes from the eye fillet, or tenderloin, which runs along the back of the lamb and is particularly sweet and tender.

2 teaspoons freshly ground black pepper

2 teaspoons salt

2 teaspoons ground cumin

2 lamb loin fillets, about 250 g (8 oz) each

extra virgin olive oil, for brushing

75 g (3 oz) watercress

250 g (8 oz) cooked beetroot in natural juices,
   drained and chopped

MINT YOGURT

125 g (4 oz) Greek yogurt

1 tablespoon chopped mint

DRESSING

1 tablespoon walnut oil, plus extra for drizzling

1 teaspoon white wine vinegar, plus extra
   for drizzling

salt and pepper

Combine the pepper, salt and cumin on a plate, brush the lamb loins with oil and dip them into the pepper mix to lightly coat the meat. Cook the lamb loin fillets in a preheated heavy-based frying pan for 3–4 minutes on each side. Wrap them loosely in foil and rest for 5 minutes.

Meanwhile, combine the yogurt and mint in a bowl and season with salt and pepper. Mix the watercress and beetroot together, dress with a little walnut oil and vinegar and arrange on plates. Slice the lamb and serve with the salad and the yogurt dressing.

Chinese steamed prawns

Steaming is the ideal cooking method for a healthy diet because it requires little or no fat and gives delicious, moist results. Marinating the prawns in rice wine, spicy aromatics, and salty soy sauce before cooking gives them a fabulous flavour.

20 raw tiger prawns, peeled and deveined

2 tablespoons Chinese rice wine or dry sherry

2 tablespoons light soy sauce

2 tablespoons water

grated rind and juice of 1 lime

2 red bird's eye chillies, deseeded and sliced

2 garlic cloves, sliced

2.5-cm (1-inch) piece of fresh root ginger,
    peeled and sliced

1 tablespoon each chopped fresh coriander,
    basil and mint

1 tablespoon groundnut oil

2 teaspoons sesame oil

plain boiled rice, to serve

Combine the prawns, rice wine or sherry, soy sauce, measured water, lime rind and juice, chilli, garlic and ginger in a bowl. Marinate for 30 minutes, if possible.

Place a heatproof plate, or layer of foil turned up at the sides, in the base of a large bamboo steamer and arrange the prawn mixture on top. Replace the lid and steam for 4–5 minutes until the prawns are cooked. Transfer to a warmed serving plate and scatter over the herbs.

Heat the groundnut and sesame oils in a small pan until smoking and immediately drizzle over the prawns. Serve at once with plain boiled rice.

Oven-baked snapper with Oriental flavours

Traditionally a whole fish would be steamed in a bamboo steamer; here, it is wrapped in foil and baked in the oven to produce a similar result – a wonderfully moist, delicately flavoured fish. Make sure the foil is wide enough to wrap the fish completely.

1.25 kg (2½ lb) red snapper, scaled and gutted
4 large spring onions, thinly sliced
25 g (1 oz) fresh root ginger, peeled and thinly sliced
2 garlic cloves, thinly sliced
100 ml (3½ fl oz) fish stock
100 ml (3½ fl oz) Chinese rice wine or dry sherry

4 tablespoons light soy sauce
2 teaspoons caster sugar
1 teaspoon sesame oil
pepper
fresh coriander leaves, to garnish
plain boiled rice, to serve

Use a sharp knife to cut 4 slashes in each side of the fish and season lightly with pepper. Place it in the centre of a large sheet of foil and pull up the edges around the fish. Top with the spring onions, ginger and garlic.

Combine the stock, wine or sherry, soy sauce, sugar and sesame oil and pour around the fish. Pull the edges of the foil together and turn them over tightly to seal the parcel.

Transfer to a baking sheet and cook in a preheated oven, 220°C (425°F), Gas Mark 7, for 25 minutes. Remove from the oven and leave to rest for 5 minutes. Carefully transfer the fish and all the juices to a large platter, garnish with coriander leaves and serve with plain boiled rice.

Chargrilled chicken with coriander salsa

To ensure the chicken is nicely chargrilled on the outside, and moist and tender on the inside, preheat the grill pan until hot, then reduce the heat to medium as you add the chicken.

2 tablespoons dark soy sauce

2 teaspoons sesame oil

1 tablespoon olive oil

2 teaspoons clear honey

pinch of dried red chilli flakes

4 large skinless chicken breast fillets, about
  200 g (7 oz) each

SALSA

1 red onion, diced

1 small garlic clove, crushed

1 bunch of fresh coriander, roughly chopped

6 tablespoons extra virgin olive oil

grated rind and juice of 1 lemon

1 teaspoon ground cumin

salt and pepper

diced tomato and steamed couscous, to serve

Combine the soy sauce, sesame oil, olive oil, honey and chilli flakes in a shallow dish, add the whole chicken breasts, cover and marinate for as long as possible.

Cook the chicken in a preheated ridged grill pan for 8 minutes on each side, until charred and cooked through. Wrap in foil and leave to rest for 5 minutes.

Meanwhile, mix all the salsa ingredients together and season with salt and pepper. Set aside to infuse. Strain the marinade juices into a small saucepan and bring to the boil, then remove from the heat but keep warm.

Serve the chicken with the couscous tossed with diced tomato and top with the salsa and the marinade sauce.

Stir-fried hoisin beans

Traditionally, the beans would be deep-fried and then cooked with the sauce, but here they are blanched to create a healthier dish. Hoisin sauce has a wonderfully deep, rich flavour.

500 g (1 lb) French beans, trimmed
2 tablespoons vegetable oil
2 garlic cloves, sliced
2 large red chillies, halved and
   deseeded
6 tablespoons hoisin sauce
1 teaspoon salt
plain boiled Jasmine rice or noodles,
   to serve

Blanch the beans in a large saucepan of lightly salted boiling water for 2 minutes, then drain well.

Heat the oil in a wok or large frying pan, add the garlic and chillies and stir briefly, then add the beans, hoisin sauce and salt. Stir-fry the mixture over a high heat for 1–2 minutes until the beans are tender and well coated with sauce. Serve immediately with plain boiled rice or noodles.

Baked vegetable frittata

For this dish, the egg and vegetable mixture is baked in the oven, rather than fried. The result is a light and savoury frittata with a wonderful flavour. Allow it to cool a little when you take it out of the oven and serve it just warm.

250 g (8 oz) asparagus, trimmed
    and halved
1 tablespoon extra virgin olive oil
2 leeks, trimmed and sliced
2 garlic cloves, crushed
2 tablespoons chopped basil
6 eggs
2 tablespoons milk
2 tablespoons freshly grated
    Parmesan cheese
salt and pepper

Cook the asparagus in a saucepan of lightly salted boiling water for 2 minutes, then drain and shake it dry. Meanwhile, heat the oil in a frying pan and gently fry the leeks and garlic for 5 minutes until they have softened. Add the asparagus and basil and remove the pan from the heat.

Beat the eggs with the milk and season with salt and pepper. Stir in the vegetable mixture and pour into a greased 1.2 litre (2 pint) ovenproof dish. Scatter over the Parmesan and cook in a preheated oven, 200°C (400°F), Gas Mark 6, for 15–20 minutes until firm in the centre. Serve warm, cut into pieces.

Pasta, rice and pizza

Spaghetti with roasted asparagus and anchovies

Make this simple, flavoursome dish when asparagus is in season and at its best. The anchovies simply 'dissolve' during cooking and impart a wonderfully subtle saltiness. You can use other types of long pasta if you prefer, such as linguine or bucatini.

375 g (12 oz) dried spaghetti

375 g (12 oz) asparagus, trimmed and cut into
   7-cm (3-inch) lengths

5 tablespoons olive oil

50 g (2 oz) butter

½ teaspoon crushed dried chilli flakes

2 garlic cloves, sliced

50 g (2 oz) anchovy fillets in oil, drained
   and chopped

2 tablespoons lemon juice

75 g (3 oz) Parmesan cheese shavings

salt

Cook the pasta in a large saucepan of lightly salted boiling water for 10–12 minutes or according to packet instructions. Drain well.

Place the asparagus in a roasting tray, drizzle with olive oil and dot with the butter. Scatter with chilli, garlic and anchovies and cook in a preheated oven 200°C (400°F), Gas Mark 6, for 8 minutes until tender.

Toss the asparagus with the hot pasta and squeeze over the lemon juice. Scatter the Parmesan over the top, season with salt and serve immediately.

Fusilli with goats' cheese
and watercress pesto

Look out for organic watercress for this twist on the classic basil pesto, which uses watercress and goat's cheese in place of the classic basil and Parmesan. Be careful not to overblend the watercress and pine nuts because the pesto is best when it still retains some texture.

375 g (12 oz) dried fusilli

50 g (2 oz) pine nuts, toasted, plus extra to garnish

1 garlic clove, roughly chopped

150 g (5 oz) watercress

7 tablespoons extra virgin olive oil

150 g (5 oz) crumbly goats' cheese, plus extra
   to garnish

salt and pepper

Cook the pasta in a large saucepan of lightly salted boiling water for 10–12 minutes or according to packet instructions. Drain well.

Meanwhile, place the pine nuts, garlic and watercress in a food processor with a generous pinch of salt. Blend for 15 seconds until roughly chopped, then blend for another 20 seconds as you drizzle in the olive oil.

Crumble in the goats' cheese and stir thoroughly. Season with pepper. Stir the pesto into the hot pasta. Divide it between 4 plates to serve and scatter with extra goats' cheese and pine nuts.

Rigatoni with courgettes, feta
and lemon thyme

Lemon thyme has a heady, floral aroma and flavour that is just wonderful in this dish. If you can't find it, use regular thyme instead and add some grated lemon rind. Grilling the courgettes on a ridged grill pan gives them a charred flavour and those professional-looking black lines, but you can fry the courgettes instead if you prefer.

375 g (12 oz) dried rigatoni

3 courgettes, cut into 1-cm (½-inch) thick slices

6 tablespoons olive oil

2 lemon thyme sprigs

2 tablespoons lemon juice

200 g (7 oz) feta cheese, cubed

12 green olives, pitted and roughly chopped

salt and pepper

Cook the pasta in a large saucepan of lightly salted boiling water for 10–12 minutes or according to packet instructions. Drain well.

Meanwhile, place the courgettes in a large bowl and toss with 1 tablespoon of the oil. Cook the courgette slices in a preheated ridged grill pan for 2–3 minutes on each side until tender.

Return to the bowl, drizzle with the remaining olive oil, scatter over the lemon thyme and squeeze over the lemon juice. Season with salt and pepper. Add the hot pasta, the feta and olives. Toss well to combine them and serve immediately.

Angel hair pasta with prawns and brandy

Small prawns are often sweeter than the big tiger prawns, and that's exactly what you want in this dish. Frozen ones are fine, just defrost them before cooking. Make sure you boil off the brandy properly to remove its slightly 'raw' taste before adding the prawns and herbs.

375 g (12 oz) angel hair pasta
25 g (1 oz) butter
4 plum tomatoes, chopped
2 tablespoons brandy
200 g (7 oz) cooked peeled prawns
3 tablespoons double cream
1 tablespoon chopped tarragon
salt and pepper

Cook the pasta in a large saucepan of lightly salted boiling water for 10–12 minutes or according to packet instructions. Drain well.

Heat the butter in a frying pan over a medium heat and fry the tomatoes for 2–3 minutes until they have softened. Pour in the brandy, turn up the heat to high and cook for 2 minutes.

Add the prawns, cream and tarragon and heat through. Season well with salt and pepper. Toss the sauce with the hot pasta and serve immediately.

Tagliatelle with spicy tuna steak

You need a very hot pan to sear tuna, and the cooking time depends on the thickness of the steak. Tuna should be served still pink in the middle, so it is better to cook the fish for a shorter time, then return it to the pan if it is not cooked to your liking. Overcooking will ruin its lovely taste and texture.

375 g (12 oz) green tagliatelle
2 large green chillies, deseeded
   and roughly chopped
25 g (1 oz) fresh coriander
   with roots
1 large garlic clove, roughly
   chopped
25 g (1 oz) almonds, toasted

2 tablespoons lime juice
5 tablespoons olive oil
4 tuna steaks, about 150 g
   (5 oz) each
salt
lime wedges, to serve

Cook the pasta in a large saucepan of lightly salted boiling water for 10–12 minutes or according to packet instructions. Drain well.

Meanwhile, place the chilli, coriander, garlic, almonds and lime juice in a blender or food processor and blend for 10 seconds. Blend again while drizzling in the oil. Season with salt. Cook the tuna in a preheated ridged grill pan or frying pan for 30 seconds on each side so it is still pink in the centre. Slice the tuna steaks in half.

Toss the hot pasta with two-thirds of the coriander sauce and divide it between 4 plates. Top each portion with 2 pieces of tuna, a dollop of the remaining sauce and some lime wedges.

Pasta shells with sausage, crème fraîche and mustard

When you need some real comfort food, go for this satisfying pasta dish. It's hearty and sustaining and makes a great winter supper or leisurely weekend lunch. Look out for good-quality sausages with loads of herbs and a high meat content.

375 g (12 oz) dried pasta shells

500 g (1 lb) Italian or herby pork sausages

1 tablespoon olive oil

2 garlic cloves, sliced

150 ml (¼ pint) white wine

1 tablespoon wholegrain mustard

200 g (7 oz) crème fraîche

pinch of grated nutmeg

salt and pepper

handful of oregano leaves or chopped
   flat leaf parsley

grated Parmesan cheese, to serve

Cook the pasta in a large saucepan of lightly salted boiling water for 10–12 minutes or according to packet instructions. Drain well.

Meanwhile, make a slit along the length of each sausage and squeeze the meat out of the skins. Heat the oil in a frying pan and fry the sausage meat for 3 minutes until it is lightly golden. Add the garlic and fry for another 1 minute.

Pour in the wine and let it bubble up, scraping any sediment off the bottom of the frying pan. Simmer for 3 minutes until the wine has nearly evaporated, then stir in the mustard and crème fraîche.

Season the sauce with nutmeg, salt and pepper, and toss with the herbs and hot pasta. Serve with grated Parmesan.

Quick mushroom and spinach lasagne

Whoever said lasagne had to be complicated? Throw this dish together for a simple supper that vegetarians and meat-eaters alike will love. Use whatever mushrooms you have – shiitake add a good earthy flavour, but chestnut mushrooms are also good.

12 fresh lasagne sheets

3 tablespoons extra virgin olive oil

500 g (1 lb) mixed mushrooms (such as shiitake, oyster and chestnut), sliced

200 g (7 oz) mascarpone cheese

125 g (4 oz) baby spinach

150 g (5 oz) taleggio cheese, derinded and cut into cubes

salt and pepper

Place the lasagne sheets in a large roasting tray and cover with boiling water. Leave to stand for 5 minutes, or until tender, then drain off the water.

Heat the oil in a large frying pan and fry the mushrooms for 5 minutes. Add the mascarpone and turn up the heat. Cook for another 1 minute until the sauce is thick. Season with salt and pepper.

Lightly oil an ovenproof dish and place 3 sheets of lasagne on it, slightly overlapping. Top with a little of the taleggio, one-third of the mushroom sauce and one-third of the spinach leaves. Repeat with two more layers, then top the final layer of lasagne with the remaining taleggio. Grill for 5 minutes until the cheese is golden.

Ravioli with burnt sage butter

Burnt butter tastes fantastic and is one of the simplest things to make, but the timing is absolutely crucial. You need only to brown the butter a little, so once you see it turning, throw in the lemon juice to stop it cooking any further.

500 g (1 lb) good-quality fresh
  ravioli
50 g (2 oz) butter
50 g (2 oz) pine nuts
15 sage leaves, sliced
2 tablespoons lemon juice
salt
grated Parmesan cheese, to serve

Cook the pasta in a large saucepan of lightly salted boiling water for 10–12 minutes or according to packet instructions. Drain well and divide between 4 warmed plates.

Meanwhile, heat the butter in a frying pan over a medium heat and add the pine nuts and sage. Stir until the nuts are light brown and the butter is pale golden. Have the lemon juice to hand and, once the butter is the right colour, turn off the heat and quickly pour in the lemon juice.

Season the butter with salt and pour over the ravioli. Scatter with Parmesan shavings and serve immediately.

Penne with chorizo, borlotti beans and peppers

This is a great standby dish that can be simply thrown together when you haven't had time to shop. Peppers and chorizo keep really well in the refrigerator, so it's always well worth having a regular supply for an impromptu meal such as this one.

375 g (12 oz) dried penne

125 g (4 oz) small chorizo sausages, thinly sliced

400 g (13 oz) can borlotti beans, rinsed and drained

300 g (10 oz) chargrilled peppers in oil, drained and sliced

75 ml (3 fl oz) white wine

small handful of basil leaves

salt

grated Parmesan cheese, to serve

Cook the pasta in a large saucepan of lightly salted boiling water for 10–12 minutes or according to packet instructions. Drain well.

Meanwhile, heat a frying pan over a medium heat and fry the chorizo for 20 seconds on each side until crisp. Add the beans and stir, until coated, in the chorizo oil. Add the peppers and wine. Simmer for 2 minutes until the wine has reduced by half.

Toss the chorizo and beans with the hot pasta and the basil. Season with salt and serve with grated Parmesan.

Smoked mackerel kedgeree

This incredibly easy dish is perfect for breakfast, lunch or dinner. Smoked mackerel is used in place of the usual smoked haddock, which needs to be poached before adding to the rice. The mackerel is much more convenient because it comes ready-cooked and has a really good, rich flavour.

3 large eggs
25 g (1 oz) butter
375 g (12 oz) smoked mackerel, flaked
375 g (12 oz) cooked basmati rice
1 teaspoon mild curry powder
4 tablespoons lemon juice
4 tablespoons chopped parsley

Place the eggs in a small pan of boiling water and cook for 7 minutes. Drain, run under cold water, peel and cut into quarters.

Meanwhile, heat the butter in a frying pan, add the smoked mackerel, rice and curry powder and toss until everything is warmed through and the rice is evenly coated. Stir in the lemon juice, parsley and boiled eggs and serve immediately.

Squid ink pasta with monkfish, chilli and spinach

Black squid ink pasta has a very subtle taste of fish and looks stunning, making it the perfect choice when entertaining friends or family.

375 g (12 oz) black squid ink pasta

25 g (1 oz) butter

200 g (7 oz) monkfish tail, cut into 2.5-cm (1-inch) cubes

2 large red chillies, deseeded and finely chopped

2 garlic cloves, chopped

2 tablespoons Thai fish sauce

150 g (5 oz) baby spinach

juice of 2 limes

salt

lime wedges, to serve

Cook the pasta in a large saucepan of lightly salted boiling water for 10–12 minutes or according to packet instructions. Drain well, add the butter and toss to coat.

Meanwhile, place the monkfish cubes on a large piece of foil and top with the chillies, garlic and fish sauce. Fold up the edges of the foil and turn them over to seal the parcel. Place on a baking sheet and cook in a preheated oven, 200°C (400°F), Gas Mark 6, for 8–10 minutes until cooked through.

Toss the contents of the parcel with the hot pasta. Add the spinach and stir until it wilts. Add lime juice and salt to taste and serve immediately with lime wedges.

Jambalaya

This Creole dish is a great way of using up leftovers, such as cold roast chicken. Oregano, which is sprinkled over the Jambalaya just before serving, is one of the few herbs that retains its flavour when dried – so if you can't find the fresh herb, use a little dried instead.

2 tablespoons olive oil
1 onion
100 g (3½ oz) frankfurters or smoked
   sausages, sliced
100 g (3½ oz) cooked chicken, cut
   into cubes
125 g (4 oz) quick-cook rice
400 g (13 oz) can chopped tomatoes
200 g (7 oz) chargrilled peppers in oil,
   drained and chopped
600 ml (1 pint) chicken stock
2 bay leaves
pinch of allspice
salt and pepper
chopped oregano, to garnish
soured cream, to serve (optional)

Heat the olive oil in a large frying pan and fry the onion for 3 minutes. Add the sausages and chicken and fry for a further 2 minutes.

Add the rice, tomatoes, peppers, chicken stock, bay leaves and allspice. Cover and simmer very gently for 10 minutes or until the rice is tender and the liquid has been absorbed.

Season with salt and pepper and scatter with oregano. Serve with soured cream, if liked.

Pasta, rice and pizza

Oven-baked beetroot risotto with blue cheese

Vacuum-packed beetroot is best for this dish – it is quick, convenient and gives a wonderful jewel-like colour to the risotto. However, be sure to choose beetroot in natural juice, not vinegar, otherwise the flavour of the dish will be spoilt.

3 tablespoons olive oil

1 red onion, finely chopped

250 g (8 oz) cooked beetroot in natural juices, chopped

200 g (7 oz) arborio or risotto rice

600 ml (1 pint) vegetable stock

150 ml (¼ pint) fruity red wine, such as Merlot

150 g (5 oz) dolcelatte or other blue cheese

salt and pepper

TO SERVE

50 g (2 oz) wild rocket leaves

25 g (1 oz) chopped pecan nuts, toasted

Heat the olive oil in a casserole dish over a medium heat and fry the onion for 2 minutes until softening. Add the beetroot and rice and stir for 1 minute, then pour in the stock and wine.

Cover with a tight-fitting lid and cook in a preheated oven, 200°C (400°F), Gas Mark 6, for 20 minutes until all the liquid has been absorbed. Stir in the blue cheese and season with salt and pepper. Divide between 4 warmed serving bowls and scatter with rocket and chopped pecans.

Aromatic Middle Eastern pilaf

This wonderful rice dish is packed with aromatic Eastern spices and makes a delicious one-pot meal – great for whoever is doing the washing up. If you're feeling like a treat, stir through some extra butter at the end for a richer, more succulent taste.

25 g (1 oz) butter
1 onion, chopped
pinch of saffron threads
2 cinnamon sticks
6 cardamom pods
75 g (3 oz) sultanas
200 g (7 oz) basmati rice
400 ml (13 fl oz) chicken or
   vegetable stock

375 g (12 oz) cooked chicken
   breast, diced
6 tomatoes, finely chopped
handful of mint leaves, shredded
50 g (2 oz) pine nuts, toasted
salt and pepper

Heat the butter in a frying pan and cook the onion for 1 minute over a high heat. Turn the heat down and add the spices, sultanas, rice and stock. Cover and cook for 5 minutes.

Add the chicken and continue to cook for 3 minutes, or until the liquid has been absorbed. Season with salt and pepper and leave for 2 minutes with the lid on. Fluff up with a fork, add the tomatoes and mint and scatter with pine nuts.

Chinese fried rice

To save time, you can cook the rice the night before or buy a packet of ready-cooked rice. You can also vary the ingredients, adding whatever vegetables you fancy, such as strips of courgette and red pepper, or cooked meat, such as ham or chicken.

2 tablespoons vegetable oil

1 carrot, peeled and finely diced

75 g (3 oz) peas

200 g (7 oz) cooked peeled prawns

400 g (13 oz) cooked basmati rice

2 eggs, beaten

1 tablespoon light soy sauce

6 spring onions, trimmed and sliced

$\frac{1}{2}$ teaspoon sesame oil

Heat a wok over a high heat until smoking. Add the oil, heat again and add the carrot and peas. Stir-fry for 2 minutes, then add the prawns and rice and stir-fry for 2 minutes.

Make a well in the centre and add the eggs. Stir the eggs for 1 minute or until lightly scrambled, then mix them with the rice and prawns. Add the soy sauce, spring onions and sesame oil and take off the heat. Mix all together thoroughly before serving.

Chicken, pea and mint risotto

Risotto cooked in the oven is incredibly simple. The final result is not usually as creamy as a risotto stirred over the hob, but this recipe includes a little cream to add at the end to make up for it. Be sure to use arborio or another risotto rice because you cannot achieve the taste and texture of an authentic risotto using any other rice variety.

25 g (1 oz) butter
1 onion, finely chopped
150 g (5 oz) skinless chicken breast fillet, cut into strips
200 g (7 oz) arborio or risotto rice
1 teaspoon fennel seeds
900 ml (1½ pints) hot chicken stock
75 g (3 oz) frozen peas, thawed
juice and grated rind of 1 lemon
2 tablespoons double cream
100 g (3½ oz) Parmesan cheese, grated
2 tablespoons chopped mint
salt and pepper

Heat the butter in a heatproof casserole and fry the onion and chicken for 3 minutes. Add the rice and fennel seeds and stir for 30 seconds, then add the stock and peas.

Cover tightly and cook in a preheated oven, 200°C (400°F), Gas Mark 6, for 20 minutes until the rice is tender and all the liquid has been absorbed.

Stir in the lemon juice and rind, double cream and Parmesan and season with salt and pepper. Cover and leave for 2 minutes, then stir in the mint. Serve immediately.

Fragrant coconut rice

This rice dish is deliciously rich and can be served as a meal in itself. Creamed coconut is sold in blocks and needs to be dissolved in water before use. Don't be tempted to use coconut cream or coconut milk because it will give rather stodgy results.

50 g (2 oz) creamed coconut
250 ml (8 fl oz) water
125 g (4 oz) basmati rice
¼ teaspoon turmeric
2 teaspoons medium curry powder
4 Kaffir lime leaves or curry leaves
1 lemon grass stalk, bruised
100 g (3½ oz) split red lentils
125 g (4 oz) baby spinach
salt and pepper

TO SERVE
200 g (7 oz) Greek yogurt
4 tablespoons chopped fresh coriander

Place the creamed coconut and the measured water in a saucepan and heat until the coconut dissolves. Add the rice, turmeric, curry powder, lime or curry leaves, lemon grass and lentils and cover with a tight-fitting lid.

Bring to the boil and simmer gently for 7 minutes until the liquid has been absorbed. Turn off the heat and stand, covered, for 3 minutes more, then stir in the spinach and season with salt and pepper.

Mix the yogurt and coriander together. Divide the coconut rice between 4 warmed plates and serve each portion with a dollop of coriander yogurt.

French bread pizzas with salami

This is a great meal for kids as well as adults, and makes a fantastic quick party dish. You can add different toppings according to your own personal taste – and the ingredients you have to hand.

1 French stick
6 tablespoons bottled tomato and basil
   pasta sauce
150 g (5 oz) mozzarella cheese, sliced
75 g (3 oz) pepperoni or salami, sliced
16 green olives, pitted and halved
1 teaspoon dried oregano

Cut the baguette in half and split each piece horizontally so you have 4 pieces. Place the bread, cut side up, on a baking sheet and spread the tomato and basil sauce over it.

Top with the mozzarella, pepperoni or salami, and olives and scatter with oregano. Cook in a preheated oven, 200°C (400°F), Gas Mark 6, for 5–6 minutes until the cheese has melted. Serve hot.

Asparagus and taleggio pizza

Taleggio is a soft and creamy Italian cheese with a slightly sweet flavour and rich, creamy texture that melts perfectly on top of the pizza. Look out for slim asparagus that will roast quickly. If you can only find large stalks, halve them lengthways before scattering over the pizza.

5 tablespoons passata (puréed
    tomatoes)
1 tablespoon (15 ml) ready-made
    red pesto
4 x 25 cm (10 inch) ready-made
    pizza bases
250 g (8 oz) taleggio cheese,
    derinded and sliced
175 g (6 oz) slim asparagus
    spears, trimmed
2 tablespoons olive oil
salt and pepper

Mix the passata and pesto together with a pinch of salt and spread over the pizza bases. Top with the taleggio and asparagus and drizzle with olive oil.

Place directly on the shelves of a preheated oven, 200°C (400°F), Gas Mark 6, and cook for 10 minutes until the asparagus is tender and the pizza bases crisp. Grind over some fresh black pepper before serving.

Tuna, caper and olive pizza

This is a cross between a pizza and a tuna melt and always feels like pure indulgence. It's perfect for a quick lunch or a late-night snack after an evening out.

1 ciabatta loaf

1 garlic clove, peeled

6 tablespoons passata or ready-made tomato pasta sauce

2 teaspoons capers

150 g (5 oz) mozzarella cheese, thinly sliced

200 g (7 oz) can tuna in olive oil, drained

¼ red onion, sliced into rings

6 green olives, pitted and halved

pepper

Slice the ciabatta in half horizontally and place the pieces, cut sides up, on a baking sheet. Cook under a preheated hot grill for 2 minutes on each side until lightly toasted.

Rub the cut sides of the bread with the garlic clove and spread with passata or tomato sauce. Scatter over the capers, mozzarella, tuna, red onion and olives.

Return to the grill for 4–5 minutes until the cheese has melted and is bubbling. Grind over some black pepper before serving.

Flatbread pizza with tomatoes and goats' cheese

Mediterranean flatbreads crisp up beautifully in the oven or under the grill, making them a perfect alternative to the classic pizza base.

4 x 20 cm (8 inch) Mediterranean flatbreads
2 tablespoons sun-dried tomato paste
300 g (10 oz) mozzarella cheese, sliced
6 plum tomatoes, roughly chopped
4 tablespoons olive oil
1 garlic clove, crushed
small handful of basil leaves, roughly torn
100 g (3½ oz) goats' cheese
salt and pepper

Place the flatbreads on 2 baking sheets and spread with the sun-dried tomato paste. Top with the sliced mozzarella and bake in a preheated oven, 200°C (400°F), Gas Mark 6, for 7–8 minutes, until the bases are crisp and the cheese has melted.

Meanwhile, place the plum tomatoes in a bowl, add the oil, garlic and basil and season generously with salt and pepper. Top the cooked pizza with the tomatoes and crumble over the goats' cheese. Serve immediately.

Pizza bianchi

The Italians love *pizza bianchi*, piled high with hot, pungent rocket leaves and a drizzle of extra virgin olive oil, rather than the usual cooked ingredients. This pizza is packed with fresh flavours and is perfect for summertime and eating outdoors.

4 x 20 cm (8 inch) Mediterranean
   flatbreads
200 g (7 oz) Gorgonzola or dolcelatte
   cheese, crumbled
8 slices of prosciutto
50 g (2 oz) wild rocket
pepper
extra virgin olive oil, for drizzling

Place the flatbreads on 2 baking sheets and scatter the centres with the blue cheese. Bake in a preheated oven, 200°C (400°F), Gas Mark 6, for 6–7 minutes until the cheese has melted and the bases are crisp.

Top the pizzas with the prosciutto and some rocket. Grind over some fresh black pepper and drizzle with oil. Serve immediately.

Spinach and ricotta pitta bread pizzas

Look out for firm ricotta for this recipe. It has a really good texture and flavour and crumbles easily. The pre-packed variety will make an adequate alternative, but it doesn't crumble as easily and you may need to spread it on the pizza.

4 wholemeal pitta breads

5 tablespoons ready-made tomato pasta sauce

150 g (5 oz) frozen spinach, thawed and
  squeezed dry

125 g (4 oz) firm ricotta cheese, crumbled

25 g (1 oz) pine nuts

2 tablespoons olive oil

salt and pepper

Place the pitta breads on a baking sheet and spread them with the tomato sauce. Top with small piles of spinach and scatter over the ricotta.

Sprinkle with pine nuts, drizzle with olive oil and season with salt and pepper. Cook in a preheated oven, 180°C (350°F), Gas Mark 4, for 8 minutes until crisp. Serve immediately.

Spicy chicken naan bread pizzas

Naan breads make great instant pizza bases and they're ready in next to no time. For an extra kick, try chilli, or another different flavour, naan bread.

4 tablespoons olive oil

1 garlic clove, crushed

2 tablespoons chopped fresh coriander

4 ready-made plain or garlic naan breads

250 g (8 oz) ready-made tandoori chicken, sliced

200 g (7 oz) cherry tomatoes, halved

¼ red onion, finely sliced

Place the olive oil, garlic and coriander in a small bowl and mix together. Put the naan breads on 2 baking sheets and scatter over the chicken, tomatoes and red onion.

Drizzle over half the oil and bake in a preheated oven, 200°C (400°F), Gas Mark 6, for 10 minutes, until the naans are just crunchy. Drizzle over the remaining oil before serving.

Oriental

Thai fried noodles

Inspired by the classic noodle dish Pad Thai, which is eaten all over Thailand, this recipe uses lime juice as the essential sour flavour – rather than tamarind, which is used in the traditional Thai version. If you want to try it with tamarind, you can buy the paste from Asian food stores.

250 g (8 oz) flat rice noodles
2 tablespoons vegetable oil
150 g (5 oz) raw tiger prawns, peeled and deveined
2 garlic cloves, crushed
1 egg, beatcn
1 carrot, grated
200 g (7 oz) bean sprouts
1 tablespoon brown sugar
3 tablespoons Thai fish sauce
2 tablespoons lime juice

TO SERVE
50 g (2 oz) peanuts, toasted
1 red chilli, thinly sliced
4 spring onions, sliced
coriander sprigs
lime wedges

Soak the rice noodles in a bowl of lightly salted boiling water for 10 minutes or until soft. Drain and set aside.

Meanwhile, heat the oil in a wok over a high heat. Add the prawns and garlic and stir-fry for 1 minute. Push them to one side and add the egg, stir until lightly scrambled and then add all the remaining ingredients, including the noodles.

Toss thoroughly until all the ingredients are well mixed and heated through. Transfer to a large serving dish and top with the peanuts, chilli, spring onion and coriander and serve with lime wedges.

Seared sesame tuna with soy and mirin dressing

This dish is wonderfully fresh-tasting and perfect for a dinner party. It also uses very little oil for cooking and is very nutritious, so you can feel doubly virtuous!

1 tablespoon black sesame seeds

1 tablespoon white sesame seeds

2.5-cm (1-inch) thick tuna steak, about 375 g (12 oz)

1 tablespoon sunflower oil

100 g (3½ oz) mixed herb or baby leaf salad

6 radishes, sliced

¼ cucumber, peeled and sliced

DRESSING

3 tablespoons light soy sauce

3 tablespoons mirin

1 tablespoon rice vinegar

½ teaspoon wasabi

Mix all the dressing ingredients together and set aside. Mix the sesame seeds on a plate, rub the tuna with the oil and roll it in the sesame seeds to coat.

Heat a frying pan over a high heat until it is smoking and sear the tuna for 30 seconds on each side until sealed and lightly golden, but pink in the centre.

Allow the tuna to rest for 2 minutes, then slice as thinly as you can. Arrange the tuna on a plate, top with the salad leaves, radishes and cucumber, then drizzle over the dressing.

Vietnamese beef pho

This is the national dish of Vietnam: a spicy, fragrant broth served with rice noodles, bean sprouts, aromatic herbs and slices of rare beef. Every mouthful tastes as though it is nurturing your body and soul, so save this comforting dish for a night when it's cold and raining outside and you feel in need of a spiritual uplift.

1.5 litres (2½ pints) chicken stock

2 lemon grass stalks, bruised

small piece of fresh root ginger, sliced

2 tablespoons light soy sauce

2 tablespoons lime juice

2 teaspoons soft brown sugar

125 g (4 oz) flat rice noodles

275 g (9 oz) sirloin steak, sliced

TO SERVE

150 g (5 oz) bean sprouts

1 red chilli, thinly sliced

handful of Thai basil leaves

handful of mint

Place the stock, lemon grass, ginger, soy sauce, lime juice and sugar in a large saucepan, bring to the boil and simmer gently for 10 minutes.

Remove the lemon grass and ginger with a slotted spoon and add the noodles. Cook according to packet instructions, adding the sliced steak for the last 2–3 minutes.

Divide the pho between 4 warmed bowls. Top with the bean sprouts, chilli, basil and mint and serve immediately.

Roasted chilli pork parcels

The Vietnamese often use lettuce leaves as a wrapper for spicy fillings. This combination of fresh, crunchy leaves and spicy stir-fried pork creates a fabulously fresh-tasting dish. If you want to try something a bit different, why not add some cooked bean thread noodles or even some freshly sliced mango to these delicate lettuce-leaf parcels.

400 g (13 oz) pork fillet

3 tablespoons dark soy sauce

2 tablespoons chilli sauce

¼ teaspoon Chinese five spice powder

1 teaspoon honey

TO SERVE

1 Little Gem lettuce, leaves separated

large handful of mint leaves

100 g (3½ oz) baby cherry tomatoes, quartered

500 g (1 lb) cooked basmati rice

Rub the pork with the soy sauce, chilli sauce, five spice powder and honey. Leave to marinate if time allows.

Line a roasting tray with foil and place the pork on top. Cover with more foil and cook it in a preheated oven, 150°C (300°F), Gas Mark 2, for 25 minutes. Remove the foil and roast for 10 minutes further until just pink in the centre. Rest for 5 minutes and then slice.

Serve all the ingredients in separate bowls and allow everyone to assemble their own rolls. Take a lettuce leaf and fill it with a spoonful of rice, a few mint leaves, chopped tomatoes and pork slices. Roll up the lettuce leaf and eat with the hands.

Warm pork and noodle salad

Using minced meat in salads is a popular technique throughout South East Asia. The pungent spices and aromatics of Eastern cuisine blend well with the meat during cooking to produce a wondrous dish packed full of flavour.

100 g (3½ oz) dried bean thread
   noodles
500 g (1 lb) minced pork
1 lemon grass stalk, finely chopped
2 red chillies, finely chopped
2 garlic cloves, chopped
2 shallots, finely chopped
shredded mint or coriander
   leaves, to garnish

DRESSING
2 tablespoons Thai fish sauce
2 tablespoons lime juice
1 tablespoon soft brown sugar

Cook the noodles in a saucepan of lightly salted boiling water according to packet instructions and drain well. Squeeze out any excess water and transfer them to a serving bowl. Mix all the ingredients for the dressing together in a bowl.

Meanwhile, heat a frying pan and add the pork, lemon grass, chilli, garlic and shallots. Fry for 6–7 minutes, stirring occasionally, until the pork is cooked and the shallots and lemongrass have softened.

Tip the pork mixture into the bowl with the noodles and pour over the dressing. Garnish with the shredded herbs and serve immediately.

Beef with broccoli, shiitake and black bean sauce

If you love black bean sauce, it is worth using fermented black beans for extra flavour. They are sold in bags and jars in Asian stores and keep well. If you're in a hurry, though, ready-made black bean sauce is still pretty tasty.

375 g (12 oz) sirloin steak, sliced
1 tablespoon cornflour
3 tablespoons vegetable oil
200 g (7 oz) broccoli, brokcn into small
   florets
150 g (5 oz) shiitake mushrooms, halved
2 garlic cloves, crushed
1 teaspoon grated fresh root ginger
2 tablespoons fermented black beans
   or black bean sauce
2 tablespoons rice wine or dry sherry
2 tablespoons soft brown sugar
3 tablespoons light soy sauce
100 ml (3½ fl oz) beef stock
salt and pepper
egg noodles, to serve

Toss the steak slices in the cornflour and season with salt and pepper. Heat the oil in a wok, add the broccoli and mushrooms and stir-fry for 2 minutes. Add the garlic and ginger and stir-fry for another minute, then push everything to the side of the wok.

Next add the steak. Stir-fry for 10 seconds and then add all the remaining ingredients. Bring to the boil, scraping any sediment off the bottom of the pan, and serve immediately with egg noodles.

Chicken teriyaki

Sake is widely used in Japanese cooking and adds a really authentic flavour. However, if you don't have any to hand, you can use dry sherry instead. Try to use Japanese-brewed soy sauce, rather than Chinese soy sauce, which has a much saltier, less malty, taste.

750 g (1½ lb) chicken breast fillets, cubed

12 spring onions, cut into 5-cm (2-inch) lengths

2 red peppers, cored, deseeded and cut
   into chunks

2 tablespoons vegetable oil

plain boiled rice, to serve

SAUCE

3 tablespoons dark soy sauce

3 tablespoons honey

3 tablespoons sake or dry sherry

1 garlic clove, crushed

3 slices of fresh root ginger

Place all the sauce ingredients in a small saucepan and simmer for 5 minutes until it has thickened. Meanwhile, divide the chicken, spring onions and red peppers between 8 pre-soaked bamboo skewers and brush with oil.

Cook the chicken skewers in a preheated ridged grill pan or under a preheated hot grill for 4 minutes on each side, or until cooked through. Brush with the teriyaki sauce and serve on a bed of boiled rice, drizzled with more sauce.

Salmon and shiitake baked parcels

You could use any fish you want for this recipe, but salmon trout goes particularly well with the taste of sake and soy sauce. Shiitake mushrooms give this dish a really earthy, savoury flavour and become silky in texture when cooked in all the buttery juices.

4 salmon fillets or salmon trout
    fillets, about 150 g (5 oz) each
100 g (3½ oz) shiitake mushrooms
8 spring onions, trimmed and
    sliced
75 g (3 oz) butter, cut into 4 cubes
4 tablespoons sake or dry sherry
4 tablespoons light soy sauce
steamed vegetables, to serve

Cut 4 pieces of foil about 25 cm (10 inches) square. Place a salmon trout fillet on each and top with the mushrooms, spring onions and a knob of butter.

Bring up the sides of the foil and drizzle over the sake or sherry. Bring the edges together and turn them over tightly to seal the parcels.

Transfer to a baking sheet and bake in a preheated oven, 180°C (350°F), Gas Mark 4, for 6–7 minutes. Open the parcels and drizzle in the soy sauce. Serve with steamed vegetables, such as pak choi, baby sweetcorn, courgettes and carrots.

Vegetable tempura with lime mayo

When frying the tempura, be careful to fill the pan only one-third full with oil because the hot oil will bubble up when you add the vegetables. To test if the oil is hot enough for cooking, drop in a tiny bit of batter. If it puffs up and floats to the surface, the oil is at the right temperature. Serve with green salad and an Asian-style dressing.

1 egg
250 ml (8 fl oz) lager
100 g (3½ oz) plain flour
¼ teaspoon bicarbonate of soda
1 large sweet potato, peeled and thinly sliced
1 small aubergine, thinly sliced
100 g (3½ oz) baby sweetcorn, halved lengthways
groundnut oil, for deep-frying
salt and pepper
green salad, to serve

LIME MAYO
6 tablespoons mayonnaise
finely grated rind of 2 limes
1 tablespoon lime juice

Mix together the egg, lager, flour and bicarbonate of soda in a large bowl and season with salt and pepper. There will be a few lumps but don't worry.

Dip the vegetables into the batter, then drop them, a few at a time, into the hot oil. Cook about 6 pieces at a time or the oil temperature will drop. Cook the aubergine slices for 1–2 minutes, and the sweet potato and sweetcorn for 2–3 minutes, stirring occasionally so that they brown evenly. Drain on kitchen paper.

Meanwhile, mix the lime mayo ingredients together and place in a small dish. Serve a platter of vegetables with the dip on the side.

Duck breasts with honey, lime and ginger sauce

This is a great dinner party dish that is guaranteed to impress guests every time. Make sure the duck skin really crisps up without burning before transferring the meat to the oven to finish cooking. The duck should be slightly pink inside.

4 duck breasts, about 200 g (7 oz) each
3 tablespoons honey
150 ml (¼ pint) white wine
finely grated rind of 1 lime
75 ml (3 fl oz) lime juice
100 ml (3½ fl oz) chicken stock
1 tablespoon finely chopped fresh root ginger
½ teaspoon arrowroot
1 tablespoon water
salt and pepper
steamed carrots and mangetout, to serve

Score the skin of each duck breast 4 times and rub generously with salt and pepper. Heat a heavy-based frying pan and cook the duck, skin-side down, for 3 minutes. Drain off all of the fat from the pan.

Transfer the duck to a roasting tray, skin-side down, and brush with 1 tablespoon of the honey. Cook in a preheated oven, 200°C (400°F), Gas Mark 6, for 5 minutes. Rest the duck for 3 minutes, then slice it diagonally.

Meanwhile, add the wine, lime rind and juice, stock, ginger and remaining honey to the frying pan and boil over a high heat for 5 minutes. Mix the arrowroot and the measured water and add to the sauce.

Bring back to the boil and spoon the sauce over the duck. Serve with steamed carrots and mangetout.

Sesame chicken katsu with soy dip

This quick-to-prepare dish is a real favourite with children, but adults will love it, too. It makes a great supper when served with steamed rice and a selection of stir-fried vegetables, or simply serve it as a fabulous hot snack with pre-dinner drinks.

4 skinless chicken breasts, about 175 g (6 oz) each
4 tablespoons plain flour
1 egg, beaten
50 g (2 oz) breadcrumbs
6 tablespoons sesame seeds
5 tablespoons vegetable oil
steamed rice or stir-fried vegetables, to serve

DIP
6 tablespoons light soy sauce
½ teaspoon grated fresh root ginger
½ teaspoon sugar
½ large red chilli, sliced

Place the chicken breasts between two sheets of clingfilm or nonstick baking paper and flatten with a rolling pin until they are 1 cm (½ inch) thick. Place the flour in one bowl, the egg in a second bowl and the breadcrumbs and sesame seeds in a third.

Dip the chicken breasts into the flour, then the egg and finally the breadcrumb and sesame mixture until they are well coated. Press on the breadcrumbs if they fall off. Heat half the oil in a frying pan and fry 2 of the chicken breasts, for 3–4 minutes on each side until cooked through. Heat the remaining oil and fry the other 2 chicken breasts in the same way.

Meanwhile, mix together the dip ingredients in a small bowl. Slice the chicken into 2.5-cm (1-inch) strips and serve with the dip, and some rice or vegetables.

Chicken chow mein

Everyone always seems to love chicken chow mein, even fussy children, which makes this classic Chinese dish a firm family favourite. It is incredibly easy to make and is a great standby meal for any day of the week, especially when you are short of time.

250 g (8 oz) dried egg noodles

2 tablespoons vegetable oil

375 g (12 oz) skinless chicken breast fillet, cut into strips

1 garlic clove, crushed

125 g (4 oz) sugar snap peas, halved diagonally

4 tablespoons light soy sauce

2 tablespoons dry sherry

200 ml (7 fl oz) chicken stock

1 teaspoon sugar

1 bunch of spring onions, trimmed and sliced

½ teaspoon cornflour mixed with 1 tablespoon water

Cook the egg noodles in a saucepan of lightly salted boiling water according to packet instructions. Drain and set aside.

Heat the oil in a wok and stir-fry the chicken for 3 minutes. Add the garlic and sugar snap peas and fry for 3 minutes. Add the cooked noodles and stir-fry for another minute.

Pour in the soy sauce, sherry, stock, sugar and spring onions. Add the cornflour mixture, bring to the boil and cook until the sauce thickens. Serve immediately.

Oriental

Monkfish and prawn Thai curry

When shopping for curry pastes, look out for those made in Thailand since these have the most authentic flavour. This recipe includes lemongrass and Kaffir lime leaves to help create a truly Thai flavour, but if you find a very good curry paste you can leave them out.

3 tablespoons Thai green curry paste

400 g (13 oz) can coconut milk

1 lemon grass stalk (optional)

2 Kaffir lime leaves (optional)

1 tablespoon soft brown sugar

1 teaspoon salt

300 g (10 oz) monkfish tail, cut into cubes

75 g (3 oz) green beans, trimmed

12 raw tiger prawns, peeled and deveined

3 tablespoons Thai fish sauce

2 tablespoons lime juice

plain boiled rice, to serve

TO GARNISH

fresh coriander sprigs

sliced green chillies

Place the curry paste and coconut milk in a saucepan with the lemon grass and lime leaves, if using, sugar and salt. Bring to the boil and add the monkfish.

Simmer gently for 2 minutes, then add the beans and cook for another 2 minutes. Take off the heat and stir in the prawns, fish sauce and lime juice. The prawns will cook in the residual heat, but you will need to push them under the liquid.

Transfer the curry to a serving dish and top with coriander sprigs and chilli slices. Serve with plain boiled rice.

Nasi goreng

This is virtually the national dish of Indonesia, where it is sold on stalls on practically every street corner and eaten any time of the day – for breakfast, lunch or dinner.

2 tablespoons vegetable oil

150 g (5 oz) chicken breast, finely chopped

50 g (2 oz) cooked peeled prawns

1 garlic clove, crushed

1 carrot, grated

$^{1}/_{4}$ white cabbage, thinly sliced

1 egg, beaten

300 g (10 oz) cold cooked basmati rice

2 tablespoons ketchup manis (sweet soy sauce)

$^{1}/_{2}$ teaspoon sesame oil

1 tablespoon chilli sauce

1 red chilli, deseeded and sliced into strips

Heat the oil in a wok, add the chicken and stir-fry for 1 minute. Add the prawns, garlic, carrot and cabbage and stir-fry for another 3–4 minutes.

Pour in the egg and spread it out using a wooden spoon. Let it set and then add the rice and break up the egg, stirring it in. Finally add the ketchup manis, sesame oil and chilli sauce. Heat through and serve, garnished with the strips of chilli.

Sweet and sour sea bream

The spicy, aromatic sauce used here is strong and perfect for livening up bland-tasting fish. You can use virtually any white fish with firm flesh, just choose medium-sized fish that are in season.

3 tablespoons plain flour

4 sea bream fillets, about 175 g (6 oz) each

4 tablespoons vegetable oil

15 g (½ oz) fresh coriander, chopped

salt and pepper

plain boiled rice, to serve

DRESSING

2 shallots, thinly sliced

2 large green chillies, thinly sliced

3 tablespoons Thai fish sauce

3 tablespoons lime juice

2 tablespoons sugar

1 garlic clove, crushed

Mix together the dressing ingredients and set aside. Place the flour in a bowl and season it with salt and pepper. Dip the sea bream fillets into the flour to coat them.

Heat the vegetable oil in a frying pan and fry the bream fillets for 2 minutes on each side. Transfer to a serving plate, scatter with the coriander and pour over the dressing. Serve immediately with boiled rice.

Indonesian baked swordfish

These tangy, spicy swordfish steaks are baked in banana leaves, which are available from Asian stores. You will need 1 large banana leaf, cut into 4 squares, plus 4 bamboo skewers for sealing the parcels. If you can't find banana leaves, use squares of foil instead.

4 swordfish or marlin steaks, about 150 g
  (5 oz) each
1 beefsteak tomato, sliced into 8
2 lemongrass stalks, bruised and cut in half
egg noodles, to serve

MARINADE

1 small onion, finely chopped
1 teaspoon ground turmeric
1 tablespoon grated fresh root ginger
2 garlic cloves, crushed
1 tablespoon chilli sauce
2 tablespoons tamarind paste

Place all the marinade ingredients in a shallow bowl, add the swordfish or marlin and turn to coat it. Leave it to marinate if time allows.

Lay 4 squares of banana leaf or foil on a work surface and place the fish and marinade on top. Top with the tomato slices and lemongrass stalks. Fold up the parcels and secure them with bamboo skewers.

Transfer to a baking sheet and cook in a preheated oven, 200°C (400°F), Gas Mark 6, for 8 minutes or until the fish is cooked through. Serve with egg noodles.

Spicy Thai squid salad

Preparing squid can be tricky, so buy it ready-prepared, if possible. You need coriander roots for the dressing, so buy the herb in a bunch rather than a packet, when the roots will have been removed. Whole prawns, slices of chicken or beef are also good cooked in this way.

1 Romaine lettuce, shredded

2 tablespoons vegetable oil

12 baby squid, prepared and cut into rings

15 g (½ oz) coriander leaves

15 g (½ oz) mint leaves

2 red chillies, deseeded and finely sliced

fried egg noodles, to serve

DRESSING

1 garlic clove, crushed

1½ tablespoons finely chopped coriander roots

juice of 2 limes

1 tablespoon soft brown sugar

2 tablespoons Thai fish sauce

Mix all the dressing ingredients together and set them aside. Scatter the lettuce over a serving dish.

Heat the oil in a heavy-based frying pan until smoking, then add half the squid. Cook for 10 seconds on each side, removing it at once to the serving dish.

Cook the remaining squid in the same way. Scatter the herbs and chillies over the squid, drizzle with the dressing and serve immediately with a dish of fried egg noodles.

Szechuan aubergine

Szechuan food is notoriously spicy and this delicious dish is no exception. When buying the yellow bean sauce, make sure you choose the regular sauce and not the concentrated variety because this will be too strong and overpowering for this recipe.

5 tablespoons vegetable oil

1 large aubergine, cut into 2.5-cm (1-inch) cubes

2 large garlic cloves, crushed

1 tablespoon grated fresh root ginger

6 spring onions, sliced

2 tablespoons chilli sauce

2 tablespoons yellow bean sauce

2 tablespoons dry sherry

2 tablespoons rice wine vinegar

1 tablespoon dark soy sauce

2 tablespoons soft brown sugar

salt and pepper

egg noodles, to serve

Heat the oil in a wok or large frying pan and add the aubergine. Cook for 5 minutes, stirring frequently so that it cooks evenly. Add the garlic and ginger and stir-fry for 2 minutes further.

Mix together half the spring onions with the remaining ingredients and pour into the wok. Stir thoroughly, season with salt and pepper and scatter with the remaining spring onions. Serve with egg noodles.

Thai chicken with basil, chilli and cashews

To make this simple Thai stir-fry, look out for Thai sweet, or holy, basil leaves, which have a slightly spicy aniseed flavour. If you can't find them, you can use fresh coriander leaves instead.

2 tablespoons vegetable oil

750 g (1½ lb) skinless chicken breast fillet,
   thinly sliced

4 garlic cloves, crushed

2 large green chillies, deseeded and chopped

1 onion, cut into chunks

1 green pepper, cored, deseeded and
   cut into chunks

5 tablespoons Thai fish sauce

2 tablespoons dark soy sauce

2 tablespoons soft brown sugar

TO SERVE

25 g (1 oz) cashew nuts, toasted

15 g (½ oz) Thai basil or coriander
   leaves

plain boiled rice

Heat the oil in a wok until smoking. Add the chicken, garlic and chillies. Stir-fry for 1 minute and then add the onion and pepper. Continue stir-frying for 5 minutes until the chicken is cooked through.

Pour in the fish sauce, soy sauce and sugar and mix well. Bring to the boil, then transfer to a serving dish. Scatter with cashew nuts and basil, and serve with boiled rice.

Chilled soba noodles with salmon sashimi

It is important that you buy exceptionally fresh, really good-quality salmon for this dish. This simple combination of flavours makes a refreshing and healthy light lunch.

200 g (7 oz) soba noodles

2 teaspoons sesame oil

1 tablespoon pickled ginger, shredded

1 tablespoon black sesame seeds

6 spring onions, trimmed and diagonally sliced

1 tablespoon lime juice

500 g (1 lb) salmon fillet, cut into 1-cm (½-inch) thick slices

soy sauce, to serve

Cook the noodles in a saucepan of lightly salted boiling water according to packet instructions. Drain and run under cold water until cool. Transfer to a mixing bowl and add a handful of ice cubes. Set aside for 5 minutes, then drain again.

Place the chilled noodles in a mixing bowl and add the sesame oil, pickled ginger, sesame seeds, spring onions and lime juice. Divide the noodles between 4 plates, with the sliced salmon, and serve with soy sauce for dipping.

Cod with ketchup manis

Ketchup manis is a thick, sweet soy sauce that is widely used in Indonesian cooking. It is available in larger supermarkets and Asian stores, but if you can't find it, you can make a reasonable substitute by blending 3 tablespoons of soy sauce and 1 tablespoon of tomato ketchup.

4 cod fillets, about 175 g (6 oz) each
6 tablespoons ketchup manis (sweet soy sauce)
1 red chilli, deseeded and finely chopped
2 tablespoons soft brown sugar
3 garlic cloves, sliced
2.5-cm (1-inch) piece of fresh root ginger,
    peeled and chopped
2 tablespoons lime juice

TO SERVE
15 g (½ oz) Thai basil or coriander leaves
steamed baby pak choi or Chinese broccoli

Place the cod fillets in an ovenproof dish and top with the remaining ingredients. Cover the dish tightly with foil and bake in a preheated oven, 180°C (350°F), Gas Mark 4, for 8–10 minutes or until the fish is no longer translucent in the centre.

Top with basil or coriander leaves and serve on a bed of pak choi or Chinese broccoli with the sauce drizzled over the top.

Aromatic chicken pancakes

If you're a fan of crispy duck with pancakes, you'll adore this variation. It has all the flavour of the authentic Chinese version, but it can be thrown together in minutes.

4 skinless chicken breasts, about 150 g (5 oz) each
6 tablespoons hoisin sauce

TO SERVE

12 Chinese pancakes
$\frac{1}{2}$ cucumber, cut into matchsticks
12 spring onions, trimmed and thinly sliced
handful of fresh coriander
4 tablespoons hoisin sauce mixed with
   3 tablespoons water

Place the chicken breasts between two sheets of clingfilm or nonstick baking paper and flatten them with a rolling pin until they are 2 cm (¾ inch) thick. Lay them on a baking sheet and brush with the hoisin sauce.

Cook under a preheated hot grill for 4 minutes. Turn over, brush with more hoisin and grill for another 3 minutes or until the chicken is cooked through. Warm the pancakes in a bamboo steamer for 3 minutes or until heated through.

Thinly slice the chicken and arrange on a serving plate. Serve with the pancakes, a bowl of cucumber, a bowl of spring onions, the fresh coriander and the diluted hoisin sauce, and allow everyone to assemble their own pancakes.

Vegetarian

Gnocchi with spinach and three cheese sauce

Ready-made gnocchi make a great alternative to pasta. For a special occasion, you could divide the little potato dumplings and the spinach and cheese sauce among individual gratin dishes and grill for 3–4 minutes until golden and bubbling.

500 g (1 lb) ready-made gnocchi
250 g (8 oz) frozen leaf spinach, thawed
250 g (8 oz) mascarpone cheese
50 g (2 oz) dolcelatte cheese
pinch of grated nutmeg
2 tablespoons freshly grated Parmesan cheese
salt and pepper

Cook the gnocchi in a saucepan of lightly salted boiling water according to the packet instructions. Drain well, and return them to the pan.

Meanwhile, drain the spinach; use your hands to squeeze out all the excess water, and chop roughly.

Stir the spinach into the cooked gnocchi with the mascarpone, dolcelatte and a little grated nutmeg. Stir gently until creamy and season with salt and pepper.

Spoon into a shallow heatproof dish, sprinkle over the Parmesan and cook under a preheated hot grill for 5–6 minutes, until bubbling and golden.

Cheesy mustard mash with roasted tomatoes

Potatoes, combined with protein ingredients, can make an excellent base for many vegetarian meals. Choose floury potatoes, such as King Edward or Desirée, because their soft, fluffy texture is best suited to mashing and will give lovely results.

750 g (1½ lb) floury potatoes, cut into small chunks

large knob of butter

4 tablespoons milk

1 small garlic clove, crushed

250 g (8 oz) Cheddar cheese, grated

1 tablespoon wholegrain mustard

salt and pepper

ROASTED TOMATOES

500 g (1 lb) small tomatoes on the vine

1 tablespoon chopped rosemary

1 teaspoon sugar

olive oil, for drizzling

Place the tomato bunches in a shallow heatproof dish and sprinkle with the rosemary and sugar. Drizzle with olive oil and season generously with salt and pepper. Cook the tomatoes in a preheated oven, 200°C (400°F), Gas Mark 6, for 15–20 minutes until lightly charred.

Meanwhile, place the potatoes in a saucepan of lightly salted cold water, bring to the boil and cook for 10 minutes or until tender. Drain well and return to the pan, then add the butter and mash the potatoes until smooth.

Return the pan to the heat and stir in the milk and garlic. Season with salt and pepper and beat gently with a wooden spoon. Gradually beat in the cheese and mustard and continue to beat over a low heat until the mixture lightens, becomes glossy and starts to pull away from the sides of the pan. Serve the mash with the roasted tomatoes.

Braised fennel with pecorino

Fennel has a delicious, light aniseed flavour that goes really well with cheese, making it ideal for a vegetarian meal. You can use large fennel bulbs rather than baby fennel if you prefer – simply cut 2 trimmed bulbs into thick wedges. You can also vary the choice of cheese – why not try Parmesan or fontina in place of the pecorino.

50 g (2 oz) butter
12 baby fennel bulbs, trimmed and
   halved lengthways
150 ml (¼ pint) water
squeeze of lemon juice
1 teaspoon balsamic vinegar
3–4 tablespoons freshly grated
   pecorino cheese
salt and pepper
boiled new potatoes, to serve

Melt the butter in a large heatproof casserole. When it stops foaming, add the fennel halves and fry gently for 2 minutes on each side until lightly golden. Add the measured water and a squeeze of lemon juice. Season with salt and pepper, bring to the boil, cover the pan and simmer gently for 20 minutes until the fennel is tender.

Remove the lid, add the balsamic vinegar and increase the heat to reduce the liquid by half. Remove the pan from the heat, add the cheese, then cover the pan again to allow the cheese to melt. Serve the fennel and pan juices with some boiled new potatoes.

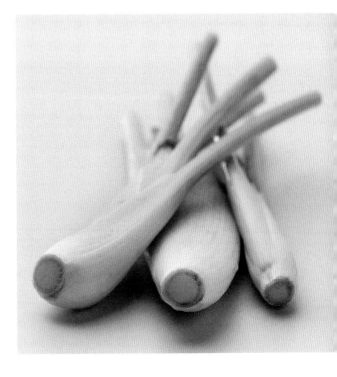

Roasted winter vegetables with soured cream and chive sauce

To make this richly-flavoured, comforting dish, you will need a large roasting tin that can hold all the vegetables in a single layer. This will allow them to cook evenly and brown all over.

1 kg (2 lb) mixed winter vegetables, such as
    carrots, parsnips, swede and turnips
12 new potatoes, halved if large
2 small onions, cut into wedges
12 garlic cloves, unpeeled
handful of thyme and rosemary sprigs
3 bay leaves
extra virgin olive oil, for drizzling
salt and pepper

SOURED CREAM AND CHIVE SAUCE
300 ml (½ pint) soured cream
1 bunch of chives, snipped

Trim the vegetables and cut them into pieces, keeping them roughly the same size as the potatoes so they will cook evenly. Place the vegetables, potatoes, onions, garlic, herbs, oil and salt and pepper in a large roasting tin and toss until well coated with oil.

Roast in a preheated oven, 230°C (450°F), Gas Mark 8, for 50–60 minutes, stirring from time to time, until all the vegetables are tender.

Meanwhile, make the sauce. Mix the soured cream and chives together and season with salt and pepper. Cover and chill until needed. Serve the vegetables with the sauce to dip.

Cheesy rosti with mushrooms and poached eggs

Crisp and golden potato cakes, topped with grilled mushrooms and poached eggs, make an elegant vegetarian supper or indulgent weekend brunch. For a special occasion, top each portion with a dollop of soured cream and a sprinkling of chopped fresh chives.

500 g (1 lb) potatoes, peeled and grated
1 onion, thinly sliced
1 tablespoon chopped fresh sage
125 g (4 oz) vegetarian Cheddar cheese, grated
5 eggs
2 tablespoons extra virgin olive oil
4 large field mushrooms
salt and pepper

Place the grated potato in a sieve and squeeze out the excess liquid. Transfer to a large bowl and add the onion, sage, cheese, and seasoning. Lightly beat 1 egg and add to the mixture, stirring well until combined.

Heat half the oil in a large nonstick frying pan, tip in the potato mixture and cook over a medium heat for 12 minutes until the underneath is browned.

Carefully slide the rosti out onto a large plate, upturn the frying pan over the plate and use oven gloves to flip the pan over, returning the rosti to the pan. Cook for a further 12 minutes until browned on the second side.

Meanwhile, place the mushrooms, cap side down, in a roasting dish, drizzle over the remaining oil, season and roast in a preheated oven 220°C (425°F), Gas Mark 7 for 20 minutes, until the mushrooms are tender.

Just before serving, poach 4 eggs in a pan of gently simmering water for 3 minutes until cooked. Serve the rosti in wedges topped with a roasted mushroom and poached egg.

Herby omelette with crème fraîche and avocado

Eggs are a great source of meat-free protein so are a valuable ingredient for most vegetarians. This sophisticated omelette topped with crème fraîche and smooth avocado makes an inspiring vegetarian meal. The omelettes are best eaten as soon as they are cooked, so make them one at a time and serve them as you go.

12 eggs
4 tablespoons chopped mixed herbs,
    such as chervil, chives, marjoram,
      parsley and tarragon
50 g (2 oz) butter
4 dessertspoons crème fraîche
1 avocado, peeled, stoned and sliced
salt and pepper

Beat the eggs with the herbs and season with salt and pepper. Melt a quarter of the butter in an omelette or small frying pan until it stops foaming, then swirl in a quarter of the egg mixture. Fork over the omelette so that it cooks evenly.

As soon as it is set on the bottom (but still a little runny in the middle) carefully slide the omelette on to a warmed serving plate, folding it in half as you go.

Repeat with the remaining mixture to make 3 more omelettes. Serve the omelettes as soon as they are cooked, topped with crème fraîche and sliced avocado.

Mediterranean goats' cheese omelette

These omelettes, filled with creamy goats' cheese and served with warm, basil-scented tomatoes, have a real taste of the Mediterranean. It's a good idea to use a combination of red and yellow cherry tomatoes for maximum colour impact.

4 tablespoons extra virgin olive oil
500 g (1 lb) cherry tomatoes, halved
a little chopped basil
12 eggs
2 tablespoons wholegrain mustard
50 g (2 oz) butter
100 g (3½ oz) soft goats' cheese, diced
salt and pepper
watercress, to garnish

Heat the oil in a frying pan and fry the tomatoes (you may have to do this in 2 batches) for 2–3 minutes until they have softened. Add the basil, season with salt and pepper, transfer to a bowl and keep warm.

Beat the eggs with the mustard and season with salt and pepper. Melt a quarter of the butter in an omelette or small frying pan until it stops foaming, then swirl in a quarter of the egg mixture. Fork over the omelette so that it cooks evenly.

As soon as it is set on the bottom (but still a little runny in the middle), dot over a quarter of the goats' cheese and cook for a further 30 seconds. Carefully slide the omelette on to a warmed serving plate, folding it in half as you go.

Repeat with the remaining mixture to make 3 more omelettes, serve them with the tomatoes and garnish with watercress.

Macaroni cheese

This hearty, warming dish includes vegetarian bacon, which is widely available in health food shops and larger supermarkets. It makes a good substitute for the real thing, but for vegetarians who prefer not to eat meat substitutes, the bacon can be omitted.

250 g (8 oz) dried macaroni
2 tablespoons extra virgin olive oil
1 onion, finely chopped
2 garlic cloves, crushed
2 teaspoons chopped rosemary
125 g (4 oz) vegetarian bacon, diced (optional)
200 ml (7 fl oz) single cream
200 ml (7 fl oz) milk

200 g (7 oz) vegetarian Cheddar cheese, grated
salt and pepper
green salad, to serve (optional)

Cook the macaroni in a saucepan of lightly salted boiling water for 10–12 minutes, or according to packet instructions. Drain well and set aside.

Meanwhile, heat the oil in a large saucepan and gently fry the onion, garlic, rosemary and bacon, if using, for 5 minutes until softened. Add the cream and milk, bring to boiling point, remove from the heat and stir in two-thirds of the cheese. Season with salt and pepper.

Stir in the cooked macaroni and divide it between 4 small heatproof dishes. Scatter over the remaining cheese and bake in a preheated oven, 230°C (450°F), Gas Mark 8, for 10–12 minutes until bubbling and golden. Cool slightly, before serving with a crisp green salad, if liked.

Spicy polenta with garlic, herbs and Parmesan

Also known as cornmeal, polenta is a staple ingredient of Northern Italy, where it is cooked with water to make a delicious savoury porridge. It can be served as an accompaniment to a stew or as a dish on its own. This version is soft polenta but it can also be baked into more of 'cake'.

900 ml (1½ pints) water

1 teaspoon salt

50 g (2 oz) butter

1 garlic clove, crushed

pinch of dried red chilli flakes

150 g (5 oz) polenta

2 tablespoons chopped mixed herbs,
    such as basil, chives, parsley and thyme

50 g (2 oz) freshly grated Parmesan
    cheese, plus extra to serve

pepper

green salad, to serve

Bring the measured water and salt to a rolling boil in a large saucepan. Meanwhile, melt half the butter and fry the garlic and chilli flakes for about 1 minute until soft but not golden. Remove from the heat.

Gradually whisk the polenta into the boiling water in a steady stream, add the garlic butter and herbs and cook, stirring, over a low heat for 8–10 minutes until the polenta has thickened and is beginning to leave the sides of the pan. Remove from the heat and beat in the remaining butter and cheese and season with salt and pepper. Spoon into bowls and serve at once, with extra cheese and a green salad.

Roasted pumpkin with walnut and rocket pesto

This flavoursome recipe is ideal for a quick lunch or supper. Choose a small, round pumpkin to make cutting easier. Any leftover pesto can be stored in an airtight container in the refrigerator for up to five days and tossed with spaghetti for a quick and simple supper dish.

1 kg (2 lb) pumpkin
extra virgin olive oil, for brushing
salt and pepper
rocket leaves, to serve

PESTO
50 g (2 oz) walnuts, toasted
2 spring onions, trimmed and chopped
1 large garlic clove, crushed
50 g (2 oz) rocket leaves
3 tablespoons walnut oil
3 tablespoons extra virgin olive oil

Cut the pumpkin into 8 wedges, discard the seeds but leave the skin on. Brush with oil, season with salt and pepper and place on a large baking sheet. Roast in a preheated oven, 220°C (425°F), Gas Mark 7, for 20–25 minutes until tender, turning it over half way through.

Meanwhile, make the pesto. Combine the nuts, spring onions, garlic and rocket in a food processor and blend until finely chopped. Gradually blend in the oils and season with salt and pepper. Serve the pumpkin with the pesto and rocket leaves.

Chinese marinated tofu salad

Light and refreshing, this salad makes a lovely starter or it can be served as part of a Chinese meal, with *Szechuan aubergine* (see page 125) or *Chinese fried rice* (see page 89), for example.

1 small cucumber, cut into
  matchsticks
1 large carrot, cut into matchsticks
150 g (5 oz) marinated tofu,
  thinly sliced
4 spring onions, finely shredded
125 g (4 oz) Chinese cabbage,
  shredded
handful of mint and coriander
  leaves
1 tablespoon sesame seeds

DRESSING
2 tablespoons sugar
4 tablespoons rice wine vinegar
1 tablespoon light soy sauce
$^{1}/_{2}$ teaspoon sesame oil
pinch of cayenne powder
pinch of Szechuan pepper

Start by making the dressing. Heat the sugar and vinegar in a small saucepan until the sugar dissolves, then simmer gently for 2–3 minutes until syrupy. Pour into a glass or metal bowl and cool slightly, then stir in the remaining dressing ingredients.

Cut the cucumber and carrot and place in a large bowl, add the tofu, spring onions, cabbage, herbs and sesame seeds. Toss well, add the dressing and stir to coat. Serve at once.

Oven-roasted mushrooms on toast

Perfect for a quick supper or late-night snack, roasting is a great way to cook mushrooms as they retain all their flavour as well as their texture. Use mushrooms of an equal size so they cook evenly.

8 large flat mushrooms
2 garlic cloves, crushed
125 ml (4 fl oz) extra virgin olive oil
2 teaspoons chopped thyme
finely grated rind and juice of 1 lemon
2 tablespoons chopped parsley
salt and pepper

TO SERVE
4 slices of buttered toast
rocket leaves
Parmesan cheese shavings

Place the mushrooms, stalk sides up, in a large roasting tin and season with salt and pepper. Put the garlic, oil and thyme in a bowl. Add the lemon rind, reserving some for a garnish, then mix together. Spoon half of the sauce over the mushrooms.

Roast the mushrooms in a preheated oven, 220°C (425°F), Gas Mark 7, for 20 minutes, until tender. Sprinkle with the parsley and drizzle over the lemon juice.

Arrange the mushrooms on the buttered toast, drizzle over the remaining oil mixture and serve topped with rocket leaves, the remaining lemon rind and the Parmesan.

Roasted stuffed peppers

Although this recipe takes up to an hour to cook, it is very quick and simple to prepare. Once it is in the oven you'll have plenty of time to relax with a drink before dinner.

4 large red peppers

2 garlic cloves, crushed

1 tablespoon chopped thyme, plus extra to garnish

4 plum tomatoes, halved

4 tablespoons extra virgin olive oil

2 tablespoons balsamic vinegar

salt and pepper

TO SERVE

crusty bread

baby leaf salad (optional)

Cut the peppers in half lengthways, then scoop out and discard the cores and seeds. Place the pepper halves, cut sides up, in a roasting tin lined with foil or a ceramic dish. Divide the garlic and thyme between them and season with salt and pepper.

Pop a tomato half in each pepper, drizzle with oil and vinegar and roast in a preheated oven, 220°C (425°F), Gas Mark 7, for 55–60 minutes until the peppers are soft and charred. Serve with some crusty bread to mop up the juices and a baby leaf salad, if you like.

Creamy lentils with celery

Like all beans and pulses, lentils are a staple in most vegetarian diets, offering a tasty source of low-fat protein. This creamy dish makes for irresistible vegetarian comfort food.

40 g (1½ oz) butter
1 onion, finely chopped
1 garlic clove, finely chopped
1 teaspoon ground cumin
1 carrot, diced
2 celery sticks, diced
2 x 400 g (13 oz) cans green lentils,
   rinsed and drained
150 ml (¼ pint) vegetable stock
2 bay leaves
125 ml (4 fl oz) double cream
salt and pepper
chopped celery leaves, to garnish
crusty bread, to serve

Melt the butter in a saucepan and gently fry the onion, garlic and cumin for 5 minutes until softened. Add the carrot and celery and fry for a further 5 minutes.

Add the lentils, stir once, and then add the stock and bay leaves. Bring to the boil and simmer for 15 minutes. Stir in the cream, season with salt and pepper and heat through. Serve garnished with celery leaves, accompanied by crusty bread.

Curried red lentils

Curry leaves are really worth looking out for because they add a truly authentic flavour to this fragrant Indian lentil dish. You will find them in most large supermarkets and Asian stores.

1 onion, chopped
2 garlic cloves, chopped
2 teaspoons grated fresh root
  ginger
3 tablespoons vegetable oil
1 tablespoon medium curry
  powder
1 teaspoon ground turmeric
½ teaspoon ground cinnamon
8–12 curry leaves (optional)

400 g (13 oz) can chopped
  tomatoes
250 g (8 oz) dried red lentils
600 ml (1 pint) vegetable stock
salt and pepper

TO SERVE

yogurt
chopped fresh coriander

Put the onion, garlic and ginger into a blender or food processor and blend until smooth. Heat the oil in a saucepan, add the onion purée, spices and curry leaves, if using. Fry gently for about 5 minutes.

Add the tomatoes, lentils and stock, bring to the boil, cover and simmer over a low heat for about 20 minutes, until the lentils are cooked and the sauce has thickened. Season with salt and pepper and serve with the yogurt and coriander.

Cannellini bean and saffron stew

Saffron imparts a lovely golden colour and distinctive flavour to this hearty, Mediterranean-style stew. If you can't find fresh bay leaves, use dried instead. However, use only one leaf because dried leaves tend to have a more intense flavour than fresh ones.

4 tablespoons extra virgin olive oil

1 onion, chopped

2 garlic cloves, crushed

1 tablespoon chopped sage

5 plum tomatoes, roughly chopped

75 ml (3 fl oz) dry white wine

1/4 teaspoon saffron threads

2 x 400 g (13 oz) cans cannellini beans, rinsed
    and drained

2 fresh bay leaves

salt and pepper

TO SERVE

freshly grated Parmesan cheese

crusty bread

Heat the oil in a frying pan or large heatproof dish and fry the onion, garlic and sage for 5 minutes until soft but not browned. Add the tomatoes, cook for 1 minute then stir in the wine and saffron and boil rapidly for 2 minutes.

Add the beans, bay leaves and salt and pepper, cover and simmer gently for 20 minutes.

Remove the lid and cook for a further 5 minutes until the liquid has reduced slightly, then season with salt and pepper. Spoon the stew on to plates, top with Parmesan and serve with crusty bread.

Grilled asparagus with feta aïoli

This sophisticated dish is perfect for summer entertaining when asparagus is in season. To trim the asparagus spears, simply snap off the tough end of the stem. The point at which they snap easily is where the tough part ends and the tender part begins.

4 bunches of asparagus, trimmed

extra virgin olive oil, for drizzling

200 g (7 oz) feta cheese, crumbled

2 garlic cloves, crushed

1 tablespoon white wine vinegar

3–4 tablespoons extra virgin olive oil

salt and pepper

boiled new potatoes, to serve

Toss the trimmed asparagus with a little oil and season with salt and pepper. Cook in a preheated ridged grill pan, or under a preheated hot grill, for 3–4 minutes, turning when half done, until tender and charred.

Meanwhile, combine the feta, garlic and vinegar in a blender or food processor and blend until smooth. Gradually blend in the oil, a little at a time, until the sauce is thin, smooth and glossy, then season with pepper.

Transfer the aïoli to a bowl and serve as a dip for the grilled asparagus. Serve with boiled new potatoes.

Coconut rice 'n' beans

Based on the classic Caribbean rice 'n' peas, this dish is similar to a risotto, but with quite different flavours. The rice is cooked in coconut milk, which imparts a wonderfully rich and creamy taste and texture. Serve it on its own or as an accompaniment to grilled vegetables.

2 tablespoons vegetable oil
1 red onion, chopped
2 garlic cloves, crushed
1 teaspoon Jerk seasoning
150 g (5 oz) long grain rice
400 g (13 oz) can black-eyed beans,
    rinsed and drained
400 g (13 oz) can chopped tomatoes
300 ml (½ pint) coconut milk
1 cinnamon stick
2 tablespoons chopped fresh
    coriander
salt and pepper

Heat the oil in a saucepan and gently fry the onion, garlic and Jerk seasoning for 5 minutes. Add the rice, stir once, and then add the beans, tomatoes, coconut milk and cinnamon. Season with salt and pepper.

Bring to the boil, cover and simmer over a very low heat for 20 minutes. Remove the pan from the heat, stir in the coriander, cover and leave the rice and beans to stand for 5 minutes before serving.

Spiced couscous salad

Couscous is a staple of North African cooking, where it is served in a similar way to rice. It has a light, fluffy texture and makes a perfect base for salads. Choose instant couscous for this recipe because it needs only to be soaked in boiling water; some types can need longer cooking times.

200 ml (7 fl oz) vegetable stock

200 ml (7 fl oz) orange juice

1 teaspoon ground cinnamon

½ teaspoon ground coriander

250 g (8 oz) instant couscous

75 g (3 oz) raisins

2 ripe tomatoes, chopped

¼ preserved lemon, chopped (optional)

½ bunch of parsley, roughly chopped

½ bunch of mint, roughly chopped

1 garlic clove, crushed

4 tablespoons extra virgin olive oil

salt and pepper

Combine the stock, orange juice, spices and ½ teaspoon of salt in a saucepan; bring it to the boil, stir in the couscous and remove the pan from the heat. Cover and let it stand for 10 minutes.

Combine the raisins, tomatoes, preserved lemon, if using, herbs, garlic and oil in a large bowl, stir in the soaked couscous and season with salt and pepper. Serve warm or allow to cool and serve at room temperature.

Morroccan rice with preserved lemon

Preserved lemons are a traditional North African condiment used to flavour rice and stews. They have a very distinctive, intense flavour and are available in larger supermarkets and Mediterranean and Middle Eastern food stores. If you can't find them, however, just omit them because their flavour cannot be replaced by any other ingredient.

250 g (8 oz) basmati rice
3 tablespoons extra virgin olive oil
1 onion, chopped
2 garlic cloves, crushed
1 teaspoon cumin seeds
50 g (2 oz) pitted black olives, roughly chopped

50 g (2 oz) semi-dried tomatoes, roughly chopped
1 tablespoon chopped preserved lemon
2 tablespoons chopped mint
50 g (2 oz) cashew nuts, toasted
salt and pepper

Wash the rice under cold water until it runs clear, drain well and transfer to a saucepan. Cover with water, add 1 teaspoon of salt and bring to the boil. Cook for 5 minutes, drain well and shake dry.

Meanwhile, heat the oil in a saucepan and gently fry the onion, garlic and cumin seeds for 5 minutes. Add the rice and the remaining ingredients, except the nuts, and stir-fry for 1 minute until all the grains are glossy.

Scatter the cashews over the rice, cover the pan with a lid and leave undisturbed for 10 minutes. Stir well, season with salt and pepper and serve.

Fragrant spring onion and ginger rice

Before cooking, wash the rice under cold water until the water runs clear; you may want to repeat the process a few times. This removes excess starch so that the grains stay separate when cooked, leaving them light and fluffy – perfect for this spicy, aromatic stir-fry.

300 g (10 oz) long grain rice

1 teaspoon salt

3 cardamom pods, bruised

600 ml (1 pint) water

2 tablespoons sunflower oil

1 green chilli, deseeded and finely chopped

1 tablespoon grated fresh root ginger

2 garlic cloves, crushed

1 bunch of spring onions, trimmed and
    finely chopped

2 courgettes, thinly sliced

2 tablespoons chopped fresh coriander

2 tablespoons light soy sauce

1 tablespoon lemon juice

Wash the rice under cold water until the water runs clear and then shake dry. Place the rice in a saucepan with the salt, cardamom pods and measured water.

Bring to the boil and simmer, uncovered, over a low heat for 5 minutes. Cover the pan with a tight-fitting lid and cook for a further 5 minutes until tender.

Heat the oil in a large wok or frying pan, add the chilli, ginger, garlic, spring onions and courgettes and stir-fry for 1 minute. Add the cooked rice, coriander, soy sauce and lemon juice, and stir over a low heat for 2 minutes. Serve hot.

Pumpkin and barley risotto

Unlike risotto rice, pearl barley does not need to be stirred constantly. As the grain cooks, it becomes tender but retains its bite, adding texture to the finished dish. You will need to buy a pumpkin at least 1 kg (2 lb) in weight to give you 500 g (1 lb) of peeled flesh.

4 tablespoons extra virgin olive oil
1 onion, chopped
2 garlic cloves, crushed
1 red chilli, deseeded and finely chopped
1 tablespoon chopped rosemary
375 g (12 oz) pearl barley
500 g (1 lb) pumpkin flesh, diced
1.2 litres (2 pints) vegetable stock
50 g (2 oz) Parmesan cheese, grated,
   plus extra to serve
50g (2 oz) mascarpone cheese
salt and pepper

Heat the oil in a large saucepan and fry the onion, garlic, chilli and rosemary for 5 minutes until it has softened. Add the barley and stir-fry for 1 minute until all the grains are glossy.

Add the pumpkin and stir well, pour in the stock and bring to the boil. Simmer over a medium heat, stirring occasionally, for 25–30 minutes, until the stock has been absorbed and the barley is tender.

Remove the pan from the heat and stir in the Parmesan and mascarpone, cover and allow to stand for 5 minutes. Season with salt and pepper and serve at once with extra Parmesan.

Fish and seafood

Roasted monkfish tail with potatoes and pancetta

Monkfish tail has a superb texture and flavour and makes a great alternative to a traditional roast. The fish is available all year round but is at its best in spring and summer. Pancetta is a type of fatty bacon, used widely in Italian cooking. It is available in supermarkets and Italian delicatessens, but you can use streaky bacon instead.

750 g (1½ lb) large new potatoes
1 large onion, cut into thin wedges
125 g (4 oz) pancetta, diced
extra virgin olive oil, for drizzling
small bunch of sage leaves
1 kg (2 lb) monkfish tail on the bone
salt and pepper

Cut the potatoes into 5-mm (¼-inch) thick slices and toss with the onions, pancetta, a little oil and the sage leaves. Season with salt and pepper, then place in a large roasting tin. Cook in a preheated oven, 220°C (425°F), Gas Mark 7, for 20 minutes.

Remove any remaining skin from the monkfish, wash and pat dry. Rub the fish with a little oil, salt and pepper. Heat a heavy-based frying pan and sear the fish for 3–4 minutes until browned all over.

Transfer the monkfish to the roasting tin, nestling it among the potatoes and onions and cook for a further 20–25 minutes until cooked through. Remove from the oven, wrap loosely in foil and rest for 5 minutes before serving the fish with the vegetables.

Tiger prawns with preserved lemon aïoli

This is a lovely summer entertaining dish, particularly if you are short of time. A large platter of juicy prawns served with a mouthwatering and unusual aïoli is guaranteed to impress.

1 kg (2 lb) cooked tiger prawns

AÏOLI

1 egg yolk
1 teaspoon lemon juice
1 garlic clove, crushed
1 tablespoon chopped preserved lemon
150 ml (¼ pint) olive oil
salt

TO SERVE

crusty bread
Little Gem lettuce salad

If you wish, peel the prawns and remove the black vein that runs down the back. Place the prawns on a large platter.

To make the aïoli, put the egg yolks, lemon juice, garlic, preserved lemon and a good pinch of salt in a food processor and blend briefly until frothy. With the blade running, gradually blend in the oil through the funnel to form a thick and glossy sauce. You may need to blend in a little boiling water to thin the sauce if it becomes too thick.

Transfer the aïoli to a bowl and serve with the prawns, crusty bread and a lettuce salad.

Salmon filo parcels

Paper-thin filo pastry dries out quickly when exposed to air, so cover any sheets that you are not using with a damp tea towel while you assemble the parcels. Wrap any leftover pastry in clingfilm and refreeze for use in another dish on another day.

8 sheets of filo pastry

4 tablespoons extra virgin olive oil

4 skinless salmon fillets, about
   175 g (6 oz) each

8 tablespoons ready-made pesto

salt and pepper

steamed asparagus spears,
   to serve

Lay 1 sheet of filo pastry on a work surface, top with a second sheet and fold in half widthways to make a rough square. Brush the pastry lightly with oil. Place 1 salmon fillet along 1 side of the pastry.

Season with salt and pepper and spread with 2 tablespoons of pesto. Fold the pastry sides over the salmon, brush these with oil and then roll up to form a neat parcel. Repeat to make 4.

Brush the parcels with oil and transfer them to a preheated baking sheet. Cook in a preheated oven, 220°C (425°F), Gas Mark 7, for 12 minutes until the pastry is crisp and golden. Rest for 5 minutes and serve with steamed asparagus.

Fish and seafood

Cheesy fish pie

Perfect for a family meal, you can make this tasty fish pie in double-quick time by cooking the pastry crust separately and assembling the pie on the plate. You could replace the whiting with any white fish, such as cod, haddock or ling.

1 sheet of ready-rolled frozen puff pastry,
   about 25 cm (10 inches) square, thawed
350 g (12 oz) skinless whiting fillets, cut into cubes
250 g (8 oz) raw tiger prawns, peeled and deveined
200 g (7 oz) frozen leaf spinach, thawed
4 spring onions, trimmed and finely sliced
1 tablespoon chopped tarragon
300 ml (½ pint) double cream
50 g (2 oz) Gruyère cheese, grated
salt and pepper
steamed broccoli, to serve

Place the whiting and prawns in an ovenproof dish. Squeeze out all excess water from the spinach, chop roughly and add to the fish with the spring onions and tarragon.

Season generously with salt and pepper, pour over the cream and top with the grated cheese. Bake in a preheated oven, 220°C (425°F), Gas Mark 7, for 25 minutes, stirring half way through, until bubbling and golden.

Meanwhile, trim the pastry sheet around the edges, prick the surface with a fork and transfer it to a preheated baking sheet. Add to the oven half way through cooking the fish mixture and bake for 10–12 minutes until it is puffed up and golden. Remove from the oven and cut into quarters.

Spoon the fish on to individual plates and top each portion with a square of pastry. Serve at once with steamed broccoli.

Mackerel with lemons and olives

Fragrant with herbs and spices, this tasty dish makes a great healthy lunch or supper. Bruising the thyme and cumin seeds helps to release their flavour. The easiest way to do this is in a pestle and mortar, or on a chopping board with a rolling pin.

4 mackerel, about 300 g (10 oz) each, gutted
    and heads removed
1 small bunch of thyme, bruised
1 teaspoon cumin seeds, bruised
2 tablespoons extra virgin olive oil, plus extra
    for drizzling
1 lemon, sliced
2 bay leaves
125 g (4 oz) black olives
2 tablespoons lemon juice
salt and pepper
tomato, basil and onion salad,
    to serve

Use a sharp knife to make 3 slashes in each side of each fish. Combine the thyme, cumin and oil, season with salt and pepper and rub all over the fish, making sure some of the flavourings are pressed into the cuts.

Arrange the mackerel in a roasting tin and scatter over the lemon slices, bay leaves and olives. Drizzle with the lemon juice and a little extra oil, season with salt and pepper and cook in a preheated oven, 220°C (425°F), Gas Mark 7, for 15 minutes until the fish are cooked through. Serve with a tomato, onion and basil salad.

Thai-style scallop salad

Sweet, tender scallops are always a treat and are perfect for entertaining. These ones are topped with crispy shallots, which are a classic Thai garnish. You can buy ready-made crispy shallots, or you can make them at home by stir-frying 4 sliced shallots in sunflower oil for 5–6 minutes until crisp and golden, then draining on kitchen paper.

1 small cucumber, thinly sliced
1 chicory head, sliced
3 spring onions, trimmed and thinly sliced
1 large red chilli, deseeded and sliced
handful each of Thai basil, coriander and mint leaves
16 large scallops, halved horizontally

extra virgin olive oil, for brushing
salt and pepper
crispy fried shallots, to garnish (optional)

DRESSING

50 g (2 oz) palm sugar, grated, or soft brown sugar
2 tablespoons lime juice
2 tablespoons Thai fish sauce
1 tablespoon water

To make the dressing, place the sugar, lime juice, fish sauce and water in a small pan and heat gently to dissolve the sugar. Simmer for 1–2 minutes until syrupy, then leave to cool.

Place the cucumber, chicory, onions, chilli and herbs in a bowl and toss well. Brush the scallops with a little oil and season with salt and pepper. Sear in a preheated ridged grill pan for 20 seconds on each side.

Arrange the scallops on plates, top with the salad and pour over the dressing. Serve garnished with crispy shallots, if you like.

Herb and Parmesan crusted cod

This is such a wonderful way to cook cod, the herb and Parmesan coating becomes deliciously crisp and golden, while the fish underneath remains beautifully moist and tender. If time is short, you can cook the fish without chilling first.

75 g (3 oz) softened butter
1 tablespoon chopped basil
2 teaspoons chopped thyme
4 skinless cod fillets, about 175 g (6 oz) each
4 tablespoons natural dried breadcrumbs
2 tablespoons freshly grated Parmesan cheese
finely grated rind of ½ lemon
salt and pepper

TO SERVE
French beans, steamed
cherry tomatoes, halved

Beat the butter and herbs together and season with salt and pepper. Spread evenly over the tops of the cod fillets.

Combine the breadcrumbs, Parmesan and lemon rind on a plate and dip the buttered side of each cod fillet into the mixture to coat well. Transfer to a foil-lined baking sheet and press any remaining crumb mixture on to the fish. Chill for 30 minutes, if possible.

Cook in a preheated oven, 220°C (425°F), Gas Mark 7, for 8–10 minutes until the fish is cooked through and the topping is golden. Remove from the oven, cover loosely with foil and rest for 5 minutes, then serve with French beans and cherry tomatoes.

Grilled lemon sole with caper and herb sauce

Lemon sole have mild, sweet flesh that is set off perfectly by the tart caper sauce. They are large fish, so unless you have a large grill pan, cook the fish two at a time.

4 lemon sole, about 300 g (10 oz) each, skinned
extra virgin olive oil spray
150 g (5 oz) butter
8 tablespoons baby capers, drained

2 tablespoons chopped parsley
2 tablespoons chopped chives
4 tablespoons lemon juice
salt and pepper
steamed carrot and courgette batons, to serve

Spray the lemon sole with oil and season with salt and pepper on both sides. Place in a foil-lined grill pan and cook under a preheated hot grill for 3 minutes on each side. Transfer to warmed serving plates, cover with foil and rest for 5 minutes.

Meanwhile, melt the butter in a saucepan and gently fry the capers for 1 minute. Add the herbs, lemon juice and pepper and remove from the heat. Pour the sauce over the sole and serve at once with steamed carrots and courgettes.

Roasted monkfish with Sicilian tomato sauce

The slightly sweet and sour flavours of this tomato sauce are typical of Sicilian cuisine. The addition of olives, capers, anchovies and pine nuts gives it a really authentic feel.

4 monkfish fillets, about 250 g (8 oz) each

3–4 tablespoons extra virgin olive oil

2 garlic cloves, chopped

pinch of dried red chilli flakes

4 ripe tomatoes, deseeded and chopped, juice reserved

125 g (4 oz) pitted black olives, chopped

2 tablespoons capers, drained and rinsed

2 anchovy fillets in oil, drained and chopped

2 teaspoons caster sugar

1 tablespoon balsamic vinegar

salt and pepper

toasted pine nuts, to garnish

crusty bread, to serve

Season the monkfish with salt and pepper. Heat half the oil in a large frying pan and fry the fish over a medium heat for 2–3 minutes until browned all over. Transfer to a roasting tin and cook in a preheated oven, 200°C (400°F), Gas Mark 6, for 5 minutes. Remove the tin from the oven, cover with foil and leave to rest for a further 5 minutes.

Meanwhile, add the remaining oil to the frying pan and gently fry the garlic and chilli flakes for 1 minute. Add the tomatoes with their juices, the olives, capers, anchovies, sugar and balsamic vinegar and simmer, covered, for a further 5 minutes until softened.

Arrange the monkfish on plates, spoon over the tomato sauce, garnish with toasted pine nuts and serve with crusty bread.

Thai fishcakes with sweet chilli sauce

You can use any firm white fish, such as haddock, cod or ling, to make these delicious fishcakes. The mixture will be slightly sticky once all the ingredients are blended, so wet your hands with cold water before shaping it into rough, flat cakes about 5 cm (2 inches) across.

250 g (8 oz) raw tiger prawns, peeled and deveined
250 g (8 oz) white fish, diced
4 Kaffir lime leaves, very finely chopped
4 spring onions, trimmed and finely chopped
2 tablespoons chopped fresh coriander
1 small egg, beaten
2 tablespoons Thai fish sauce
65 g (2½ oz) rice flour
sunflower oil, for frying
lime wedges, to garnish
sweet chilli sauce, to serve

Place all the ingredients, except the sunflower oil, in a blender or food processor and pulse briefly until blended. Use wet hands to shape the mixture into 12 flat cakes.

Heat 1 cm (½ inch) of sunflower oil in a frying pan and fry the cakes in batches for 2 minutes on each side until golden.

Drain on kitchen paper and keep warm in a low oven while cooking the remainder. Garnish with lime wedges and serve with sweet chilli sauce for dipping.

Coconut steamed fish parcels

In Thailand, these fish parcels would traditionally be wrapped in banana leaves, but foil can be used instead. They would also be cooked over coals, so barbecue the parcels if you prefer.

4 skinless haddock fillets, about 200 g (7 oz) each
2 teaspoons sesame oil
2.5-cm (1-inch) piece of fresh root ginger, peeled
  and cut into thin strips
1 long red chilli, deseeded and thinly sliced
1 garlic clove, sliced
4 Kaffir lime leaves, finely shredded
1 bunch of fresh coriander
200 ml (7 fl oz) coconut milk
1½ tablespoons Thai fish sauce
2 tablespoons lime juice
salt and pepper
plain boiled rice, to serve

Lightly season the haddock fillets with salt and pepper and lay each one in the centre of a large foil square. Drizzle over the sesame oil. Combine the ginger, chilli, garlic and lime leaves and scatter over the fish.

Carefully pull up the edges of the foil parcels and add a coriander sprig to each one. Mix the coconut milk, fish sauce and lime juice together, divide between the parcels and seal the edges of the foil tightly together.

Place the parcels on a baking sheet and cook in a preheated oven, 200°C (400°F), Gas Mark 6, for 10 minutes. Remove from the oven and rest for 5 minutes. Transfer the fish and juices to warmed plates, scatter over some chopped coriander and serve with boiled rice.

Baked trout with horseradish tartare

The addition of fresh horseradish gives this tartare sauce a fabulous bite. If you can't get fresh horseradish, use bottled grated horseradish or creamed horseradish instead.

4 rainbow trout, about 300 g
   (10 oz) each, gutted
1 lemon, sliced
a few herb sprigs, such as dill,
   oregano and parsley
olive oil, for brushing
salt and pepper
lemon wedges, to garnish
boiled new potatoes, to serve

HORSERADISH TARTARE SAUCE
200 ml (7 fl oz) mayonnaise
1 tablespoon grated fresh
   horseradish
1 small shallot, finely chopped
1 tablespoon chopped mixed
   herbs, such as chives, parsley
   and tarragon
2 tablespoons capers, drained,
   rinsed and finely chopped

Wash and dry the trout inside and out and fill each cavity with lemon slices and herb sprigs. Place the fish on a foil-lined baking sheet, brush with oil and rub the skin with salt and pepper.

Cook in a preheated oven, 200°C (400°F), Gas Mark 6, for 15–18 minutes or until just cooked through. Remove from the oven, cover with foil and rest for 5 minutes.

Meanwhile, combine all the ingredients for the sauce in a bowl and season with salt and pepper. Garnish the trout with lemon wedges and serve with the horseradish tartare sauce and new potatoes.

Grilled snapper with salmoriglio

Red snapper are stunning fish and will always make an impact at a dinner party. Served with the classic Italian garlic and lemon sauce, salmoriglio, your guests cannot fail to be impressed. Serve with plenty of crusty bread to mop up the delicious juices.

4 red snapper, about 350 g (12 oz) each,
   scaled and gutted, head and tail removed
150 ml (¼ pint) extra virgin olive oil
4 tablespoons lemon juice
2 garlic cloves, crushed
2 tablespoons chopped parsley
1 teaspoon dried oregano
salt and pepper

TO SERVE
tomato, red onion, olive and basil salad
crusty bread

Use a sharp knife to make 4 slashes in each side of each fish. Season with salt and pepper and brush all over with a little of the olive oil. Cook the fish in a preheated ridged grill pan or under a preheated hot grill for 5–7 minutes on each side until they are cooked through.

Meanwhile, whisk the remaining oil, the lemon juice, garlic and herbs together in a bowl and season with salt and pepper. Transfer the cooked fish to a large warmed platter and spoon over the sauce, cover with foil and rest for 5 minutes.

Serve the red snapper with a tomato, red onion, olive and basil salad with plenty of crusty bread.

Italian steamed clams

Try to find tiny vongole clams for this dish because they are deliciously tender and juicy.
Mussels could be used instead, but they will need to be cooked for about 1 minute longer.

100 ml (3½ fl oz) extra virgin olive oil
4 garlic cloves, sliced
pinch of dried red chilli flakes
2 kg (4 lb) clams, scrubbed
100 ml (3½ fl oz) dry white wine
juice of 1–2 lemons
1 small bunch of parsley, chopped
ciabatta or French bread, to serve
salt and pepper

Heat the oil in a large saucepan and gently fry the garlic and chilli flakes with a little salt and pepper for 1 minute, until soft but not golden.

Add the clams, wine and a squeeze of lemon juice, cover and cook over a medium heat for 3–4 minutes or until all the clams have opened, shaking the pan occasionally. Discard any clams that remain closed.

Remove the pan from the heat, scatter over the parsley and add more lemon juice, to taste. Spoon into bowls and serve with bread to mop up the juices.

Fried squid with barbecue sauce

Ready-cleaned squid are widely available, which makes preparation so much quicker. Squid that are about 20 cm (8 inches) long are perfect for this dish. Be careful not to overcook them because they can become rubbery when cooked for too long.

4 squid, about 750 g (1 ½ lb) total weight

1 tablespoon sunflower oil

½ teaspoon salt

¼ teaspoon Chinese five spice powder

2 tablespoons sweet chilli sauce

1 tablespoon sweet soy sauce

1 garlic clove, crushed

2 tablespoons lime juice

TO SERVE

dressed green salad

crusty bread

Cut the squid in half, wash and pat dry. Cut each piece crossways into thick slices and toss with the oil, salt and spice powder. Mix the remaining ingredients in a bowl.

Heat a large frying pan until hot and stir-fry half the squid for about 2 minutes until golden, transfer to a plate and cook the remaining squid.

Return all the squid to the pan, add the sauce and cook, stirring, for about 1 minute until all the squid is glazed. Spoon the squid on to warmed plates and serve with salad and crusty bread.

Roasted cod with prosciutto, cherry tomatoes and olives

All-in-one dishes are great for mid-week entertaining, but this attractive dish is tasty enough to grace the table of any dinner party.

375 g (12 oz) cherry tomatoes, halved

50 g (2 oz) pitted black olives

2 tablespoons capers, drained and rinsed

grated rind and juice of 1 lemon

2 teaspoons chopped thyme

4 tablespoons extra virgin olive oil

4 cod fillets, about 175 g (6 oz) each

4 slices of prosciutto

salt and pepper

basil leaves, to garnish

TO SERVE

new potatoes

green salad

Combine the tomatoes, olives, capers, lemon rind, thyme and oil in a roasting tin and season with salt and pepper. Fit the cod fillets into the pan, spooning some of the tomato mixture over the fish.

Scatter the ham over the top and roast in a preheated oven, 220°C (425°), Gas Mark 7, for 15 minutes. Remove the tin from the oven, drizzle over the lemon juice, cover with foil and rest for 5 minutes.

Garnish the cod with basil leaves and serve with new potatoes and a green salad.

Thai-style curried mussels

Farmed mussels are available all year round and tend to be cleaner than wild mussels, making them quicker to prepare. Check the mussels before cooking: discard any open ones that do not close when sharply tapped. After cooking, throw out any mussels that remain closed.

1 tablespoon sunflower oil
2 teaspoons Thai red curry paste
8 Kaffir lime leaves, bruised
2 lemon grass stalks, roughly chopped
2 kg (4 lb) farmed mussels, washed
400 ml (14 fl oz) coconut milk
1 tablespoon Thai fish sauce
1 tablespoon lime juice
1 tablespoon caster sugar
plain boiled rice, to serve

TO GARNISH
sliced red chilli
coriander leaves
shredded Kaffir lime leaves

Heat the oil in a wok or large saucepan and gently fry the curry paste, lime leaves and lemon grass for 1 minute until fragrant.

Add the mussels with a splash of cold water, cover and cook for 4 minutes, shaking the pan several times. Remove the lid, add the remaining ingredients, stirring well, cover and cook for a further 2 minutes, until all the mussels have opened. Discard any that remain closed.

Spoon the mussels into serving bowls, strain over the sauce and garnish with the chilli, coriander and lime leaves. Serve with a bowl of plain rice.

Seared scallops with preserved lemon salsa

Try to buy scallops that have not been pre-soaked because their flavour will be better. They should look almost translucent, not white or cream. Reserve the corals of the scallops and freeze them for later use in making a fish stock or sauce.

40 g (1½ oz) preserved lemon, finely diced
40 g (1½ oz) sun-dried tomatoes, finely diced
3 small shallots, finely chopped
1 tablespoon chopped basil
5 tablespoons extra virgin olive oil
20 large scallops, corals removed
salt and pepper

TO SERVE
salad leaves
crusty bread

Combine the preserved lemon, sun-dried tomatoes, shallots, basil and 3 tablespoons of the oil in a bowl and season with salt and pepper. Toss the scallops with the remaining oil and season with salt and pepper.

Cook the scallops in a preheated ridged grill pan for 1 minute on each side. Make a bed of salad leaves on each of 4 plates and top with the scallops. Add a little of the salsa and serve at once with crusty bread.

Swordfish with sage pangritata and green beans

Pangritata is an Italian mixture of golden breadcrumbs and garlic fried in olive oil. Scattered over the seared swordfish and lightly cooked green beans, it adds a lovely flavour and texture to the dish.

5 tablespoons extra virgin olive oil,
  plus extra to serve
2 garlic cloves, chopped
2 tablespoons chopped sage leaves
125 g (4 oz) fresh white breadcrumbs
grated rind and juice of 1 lemon
250 g (8 oz) fine green beans
4 swordfish fillets, about
  200 g (7 oz) each

Heat 4 tablespoons of the oil in a frying pan and fry the garlic, sage, breadcrumbs and lemon rind, stirring constantly, for 5 minutes until crisp and golden. Drain thoroughly on kitchen paper.

Cook the beans in a pan of lightly salted boiling water for 3 minutes until just tender, drain well, season with salt and pepper and toss with a little lemon juice. Keep warm.

Meanwhile, brush the swordfish with oil, season with salt and pepper and sear in a preheated ridged grill pan for 1½ minutes on each side. Remove from pan, cover with foil and rest briefly.

Transfer the swordfish to individual plates, drizzle with lemon juice and top with the breadcrumbs. Serve with the beans and drizzle with extra virgin olive oil.

Finger-licking garlic prawns

This dish is deliciously rich and buttery, but you can replace the butter with 100 ml (3½ fl oz) of extra virgin olive oil if you prefer. Devein the prawns by cutting down the back of each one with a sharp knife and removing the black cord.

100 g (3½ oz) butter
2 garlic cloves, crushed
24 raw tiger prawns, peeled and deveined
1 tablespoon chopped parsley
2 tablespoons lemon juice
salt and pepper
crusty bread, to serve

Melt the butter in a large frying pan, add the garlic and fry gently for 30 seconds. Add the prawns, season with salt and pepper and cook over a low heat for about 3 minutes, until the prawns are just cooked through, turning them half way through.

Remove the pan from the heat and stir in the parsley and lemon juice. Allow the prawns to cool slightly, and serve with crusty bread to mop up the juices.

Seared tuna with crushed potatoes and watercress

This simple dish is great for either a casual supper or a more formal dinner. The potatoes are only half-mashed so that they retain some chunky texture. For the best results, choose a waxy potato, such as new potatoes or salad potatoes.

6 tablespoons extra virgin olive oil, plus
    extra to serve
2 teaspoons chopped thyme
grated rind of 1 lemon
4 tuna steaks, about 200 g (7 oz) each
750 g (1½ lb) new potatoes, scrubbed
2 garlic cloves, crushed
50 g (2 oz) watercress leaves
salt and pepper

Mix 2 tablespoons of the oil with the thyme and lemon rind and season with salt and pepper. Rub all over the tuna and leave to marinate until required. Cook the potatoes in a saucepan of lightly salted water for 12–15 minutes or until just tender.

Heat the remaining oil in a small frying pan and fry the garlic for 3–4 minutes until soft, but not golden. Drain the potatoes, return to the pan and use a potato masher to lightly crush the potatoes with the garlic oil. Season with salt and pepper and keep warm.

Cook the tuna steaks in a preheated ridged grill pan for 45 seconds on each side, wrap in foil and rest for 5 minutes. Stir the watercress into the potatoes to wilt slightly, spoon on to plates and serve topped with the tuna.

Sea bass with roasted fennel and salsa verde

Salsa verde is Italian for green sauce. The rich, herby flavours make it the perfect accompaniment to grilled meat and fish. The sea bass is cooked on top of the fennel, adding maximum flavour.

2 fennel bulbs, trimmed
1 large red onion, sliced
2 tablespoons extra virgin olive oil
4 sea bass fillets, about 175 g
    (6 oz) each
1 lemon, halved
salt and pepper

SALSA VERDE

1 tablespoon capers, drained
    and rinsed
1 bunch of flat leaf parsley
½ bunch of dill
1 garlic clove, chopped
1 teaspoon Dijon mustard
2 teaspoons white wine vinegar
150 ml (¼ pint) extra virgin
    olive oil

Discard the tough outer layer of fennel, reserving any fronds, and slice each bulb thinly. Combine the fennel slices, reserved fronds, onion and oil in a roasting tin and season with salt and pepper. Cook in a preheated oven, 220°C (425°), Gas Mark 7, for 30 minutes, until the vegetables are tender.

Meanwhile, place all the ingredients for the salsa verde, except the oil, in a blender or food processor and blend until roughly chopped. Gradually blend in enough oil to form a sauce and season with salt and pepper.

Season the sea bass fillets with salt and pepper, then place them, skin side up, over the cooked fennel. Squeeze over some lemon juice, drizzle with a little extra oil and bake for 5 minutes until the fish is cooked. Rest for 5 minutes, and serve the fish and vegetables with the salsa verde.

Five spice salmon with Asian greens

Chinese five spice powder is a ready-made blend of Szechuan peppercorns, cassia or cinnamon, cloves, fennel seeds and star anise and gives this dish an unmistakable Asian flavour. Shao Hsing is a Chinese rice wine, which is available from specialist Chinese food stores, but you can use dry sherry or another rice wine as an alternative.

2 teaspoons crushed black pepper

2 teaspoons Chinese five spice powder

1 teaspoon salt

$^{1}/_{4}$ teaspoon cayenne pepper

4 salmon fillets, about 200 g (7 oz) each, skinned

3 tablespoons sunflower oil

500 g (1 lb) choi sum or pak choi, sliced

3 garlic cloves, sliced

3 tablespoons Shao Hsing wine or dry sherry

75 ml (3 fl oz) vegetable stock

2 tablespoons light soy sauce

1 teaspoon sesame oil

plain boiled rice, to serve

Combine the pepper, five spice powder, salt and cayenne. Brush the salmon with a little of the oil and dust with the spice coating. Cook the fish in a preheated ridged grill pan, for 4 minutes, turn and cook for a further 2–3 minutes until the fish is just cooked through. Transfer to a plate, cover with foil and rest for 5 minutes.

Meanwhile, heat the remaining oil in a wok, add the greens and stir-fry for 2 minutes, add the garlic and stir-fry for a further 1 minute. Add the wine or sherry, stock, soy sauce and sesame oil and cook for a further 2 minutes until the greens are tender. Serve the salmon and greens with a bowl of boiled rice.

Meat and poultry

Roast chicken with lemon, rosemary and garlic butter

A modern twist to an old favourite. Here, a plain chicken is dressed up with lemon and garlic-speckled butter spread over it just before roasting with baby new potatoes and lemon wedges. No need to make gravy, just serve with a drizzle of meat juices and a light rocket salad.

1.5 kg (3 lb) oven-ready chicken

2 lemons

10 cloves garlic

small bunch rosemary, chopped

50 g (2 oz) butter

750 g (1 ½ lb) baby new potatoes

2 sweet potatoes, cut into chunks

salt and pepper

rocket salad, to serve

Place the chicken in a large roasting tin. Finely grate 1 lemon, then cut both of the lemons into wedges. Crush 2 cloves of garlic and put the rest aside. Beat the chopped rosemary, grated lemon rind, crushed garlic, salt and pepper into the butter. Spread two-thirds of the butter over the chicken, then tuck a few lemon wedges inside and on top of the chicken. Loosely cover the chicken with foil and bake in a preheated oven, 190°C (375°F), Gas Mark 5, for 1 hour.

Remove the foil, spoon over the pan juices then add the potatoes, sweet potatoes, remaining lemon wedges and garlic. Roast for 30–40 minutes until the chicken is cooked, turning the potatoes once so that they brown evenly. Spread the chicken with the remaining rosemary butter before serving with a rocket salad.

Pork schnitzel

Schnitzel was originally made with veal, but thinly sliced pork loin chops work just as well. They make a great family supper flavoured with a little grated Parmesan and served with a wonderfully fresh basil and caper sauce.

8 thin slices of pork loin, about 750 g (1½ lb) in total

2 eggs, beaten

100 g (3½ oz) fresh breadcrumbs

3 tablespoons freshly grated Parmesan cheese

3 tablespoons olive oil

125 g (4 oz) Greek yogurt

1 tablespoon capers, drained and rinsed

fincly grated rind of ½ lemon

small handful of basil leaves

salt and pepper

TO SERVE

boiled new potatoes

steamed green beans

Trim any fat from the pork. Mix the beaten eggs with salt and pepper in a shallow dish. Then, mix the breadcrumbs and Parmesan together in another shallow dish. Dip each pork slice first into the egg and then into the crumbs until coated on both sides.

Heat 2 tablespoons of the oil in a large frying pan, add half the pork slices and fry for 5 minutes, turning once or twice, until golden and thoroughly cooked. Remove from the pan and keep warm. Add the remaining oil and pork and cook in the same way.

Meanwhile, mix the yogurt with the capers, lemon rind, a few torn basil leaves, salt and pepper. Garnish the cooked pork with the remaining basil leaves and serve with the yogurt sauce, new potatoes and green beans.

Lamb pimenton

Unlike some chilli powders, Spanish pimenton has a mellow heat and a wonderful smoky taste that complements the tender lamb and earthy flavour of the new potatoes. This dish tastes great the next day, so keep any leftovers in the refrigerator and simply reheat.

1 tablespoon olive oil

2 lamb fillets, about 500 g (1lb) in total, thinly sliced

1 onion, chopped

2 garlic cloves, chopped

1 red pepper, cored, deseeded and cut into strips

1 orange pepper, cored, deseeded and cut into strips

1¼ teaspoons pimenton (smoked hot paprika)

2 tablespoons plain flour

425 g (14 oz) can chopped tomatoes

300 ml (½ pint) chicken stock

100 g (3½ oz) stoned black olives

500 g (1 lb) new potatoes, cut in half if large

handful of oregano or rosemary sprigs, plus extra to garnish

salt and pepper

crusty bread, to serve

Heat the oil in a large frying pan and add the lamb, a few pieces at a time. Cook over a high heat until just beginning to brown. Add the onion and garlic and fry until softened.

Stir in the peppers with the pimenton, cook for 1 minute then mix in the flour. Add the tomatoes, stock, olives and potatoes. Season with salt and pepper and add the herb sprigs.

Bring to the boil, transfer to a heatproof casserole dish, cover and cook in a preheated oven, 180°C (350°F), Gas Mark 4, for 1½ hours, until the potatoes are tender. Stir well and garnish with extra herbs. Serve with crusty bread to mop up the sauce.

Blue cheese and chicken wraps

Tender chicken breasts stuffed with creamy Gorgonzola and sun-dried tomatoes, then wrapped in wafer-thin slices of Serrano ham, make a great meal for friends or family. The chicken wraps can be prepared ahead of time and popped in the oven just before you're ready to eat. For a slightly milder-tasting dish, use brie, Camembert or Cheddar instead of blue cheese.

4 skinless, boneless chicken breasts, about 150 g
(5 oz) each
125 g (4 oz) Gorgonzola cheese, cut into 4 pieces
4 sun-dried tomatoes in oil, drained
4 slices of Serrano ham, about 50 g (2 oz) in total
2 tablespoons olive oil
salt and pepper

TO SERVE
griddled asparagus
griddled tomatoes on the vine

Cut a slit through the side of each chicken breast and enlarge it to make a small pocket. Tuck a piece of cheese and a sun-dried tomato into each pocket, season with salt and pepper, then wrap each breast in a slice of ham.

Put the chicken breasts, the join in the ham downwards, on a foil-lined baking sheet. Drizzle with the oil, then cook in a preheated oven, 190°C (375°F), Gas Mark 5, for 18–20 minutes until the ham has darkened and the chicken is cooked through. Transfer to individual plates and serve with griddled asparagus and tomatoes.

Pork medallions with sherried figs

Look out for extra trimmed, lean pork loin steaks, or medallions, in the supermarket, they are ideal for this deliciously easy Italian-style dish. The meat is complemented by the alcohol flavours – sherry or Marsala – and the sliced figs and golden fried onions.

2 tablespoons olive oil

8 pork medallions, about 675 g (1 lb 6 oz)

2 onions, thinly sliced

2 garlic cloves, crushed

150 g (5 oz) ready-to-eat dried figs, thickly sliced

125 ml (4 fl oz) cream sherry or Marsala

300 ml (½ pint) chicken stock

3 teaspoons thick honey

2 tablespoons crème fraîche

salt and pepper

flat leaf parsley sprigs and paprika, to garnish

buttered soft polenta, to serve

Heat the oil in a large frying pan, add the pork medallions and cook over a high heat until browned on one side. Turn the pork over and add the onions and garlic. Fry for 5 minutes, turning the pork once or twice and stirring the onions until both are browned.

Add the figs with the sherry or Marsala, stock, honey and season with salt and pepper. Cook over a moderate heat for 5 minutes until the sauce has reduced and the pork is thoroughly cooked. Stir in the crème fraîche. Garnish with torn parsley leaves and a little paprika and serve on a bed of polenta.

Peppered beef fillet with horseradish potatoes

Perfect for an extra special occasion, this pepper-crusted beef fillet is roasted above a dish of creamy, garlicky potatoes, pepped up with some horseradish sauce. As the potatoes are fairly rich, serve this dish simply with a watercress salad.

625 g (1¼ lb) baking potatoes, scrubbed and
    thinly sliced
2 garlic cloves, crushed
300 ml (½ pint) double cream
1 tablespoon horseradish cream
pinch of grated nutmeg
15 g (½ oz) butter
2 tablespoons mixed coloured peppercorns,
    crushed
675 g (1 lb 6 oz) beef fillet
1 tablespoon olive oil
salt and pepper
watercress salad, to serve

Cook the potatoes in a saucepan of lightly salted water for 5 minutes until just tender. Drain and arrange in a shallow ovenproof dish. Mix the garlic with the cream, horseradish cream and nutmeg and season with salt and pepper. Pour over the potatoes and dot with the butter.

Press the peppercorns on to the outside of the beef fillet. Place it in a small oiled roasting tin and drizzle with the rest of the oil. Cook the beef and potatoes in a preheated oven, 200°C (400°), Gas Mark 6, for 20 minutes for rare, 25 minutes for medium and 30 minutes for well done, with the beef on the top shelf and potatoes below.

Leave to stand for 5 minutes then slice the beef thinly and arrange on plates with the meat juices drizzled over. Serve with the potatoes and a watercress salad.

Meat and poultry

Cheat's Guinness pie

Guinness adds a certain rich malty taste to a beef casserole, but you can use another brand of stout ale if you prefer. Cooking the puff pastry topping separately saves on time and effort and your guests will never know the difference.

1 sheet of ready-rolled frozen puff pastry, about 25 cm (10 inches) square, thawed
beaten egg, for brushing
1 small bunch of thyme
1 tablespoon sunflower oil
750 g (1½ lb) stewing beef, diced
1 onion, chopped
250 g (8 oz) cup mushrooms, quartered
2 tablespoons plain flour
325 ml (12 fl oz) Guinness or other stout ale
200 ml (7 fl oz) beef stock

1 tablespoon tomato purée
1 tablespoon brown sugar
2 teaspoons Dijon mustard
coarse sea salt and pepper

TO SERVE

steamed green beans and baby carrots

Cut the pastry into 4 and arrange on an oiled baking sheet. Mark diagonal lines across the top of each with a knife, brush with beaten egg and sprinkle with a little salt and a few thyme leaves. Bake in a preheated oven, 200°C (400°F), Gas Mark 6, for 10 minutes until golden brown.

Meanwhile, heat the oil in a frying pan, add the beef and cook over a high heat, stirring, until just beginning to brown. Add the onion and cook for 5 minutes. Add the mushrooms, stir them into the pan, then mix in the flour.

Stir in the Guinness or stout ale, stock, tomato purée, sugar, mustard and 3 or 4 thyme sprigs. Season and bring to the boil, then transfer to a heatproof casserole dish. Reduce the oven temperature to 180°C (350°F), Gas Mark 4, and let the beef cook for 1½ hours.

Reheat the pastry in the oven for 5 minutes, then spoon the beef on to plates and top with pastry lids and sprinkle with the remaining thyme leaves. Serve with green beans and baby carrots.

One-pan spiced pork

Great for no-fuss entertaining: you can simply place the pork chops in a roasting tin with the other ingredients and leave them to bake while you enjoy a drink and nibbles with your guests, safe in the knowledge that the dinner will look after itself.

4 loin pork chops, about 175 g (6 oz) each

3 parsnips, cut into chunks

1 butternut squash, peeled, deseeded and
   thickly sliced

2 red-skinned dessert apples, cored
   and quartered

1 teaspoon fennel seeds

2 teaspoons coriander seeds

2 garlic cloves, chopped

1 teaspoon turmeric

3 tablespoons olive oil

1 tablespoon clear honey

salt and pepper

Snip through the fat on the rind of the pork chops so that they do not curl up during cooking. Place them in a large roasting tin with the parsnips, squash and apples.

Crush the fennel and coriander seeds with a pestle and mortar, then mix with the garlic, turmeric, oil and honey. Season with salt and pepper and brush the mixture over the pork and vegetables.

Cook in a preheated oven, 190°C (375°F), Gas Mark 5, for 35–40 minutes, turning the vegetables once, until golden brown and tender. Spoon on to warmed plates and serve.

Slow-cooked lamb shanks with juniper

Flavoured with orange, juniper, bay leaves and red wine, this is definitely a dish for those with a hearty appetite. Lamb shanks are really meaty, and long, slow cooking produces fabulously tender, juicy results. Mash of any kind is a perfect partner to such wondrous meat.

2 tablespoons olive oil

4 lamb shanks, about 875 g (1¾ lb) in total

2 onions, chopped

3 tablespoons plain flour

300 ml (½ pint) red wine

600 ml (1 pint) lamb or chicken stock

finely grated rind of 1 orange, plus extra to garnish

2 teaspoons juniper berries, crushed

½ teaspoon ground cinnamon

4 fresh bay leaves, plus extra to garnish

salt and pepper

mashed parsnips or celeriac, to serve

Heat the oil in a large flameproof pan, add the lamb and cook until browned on one side. Turn the lamb shanks over and add the onion to the pan. Continue cooking until the lamb is browned on all sides and the onion is softened.

Stir the flour into the pan, then gradually mix in the wine and stock. Add the orange rind, juniper, cinnamon and bay leaves and season with salt and pepper. Bring to the boil, stirring, then pour over the lamb.

Cover the pan and cook in a preheated oven, 160°C (325°F), Gas Mark 3, for 3 hours, turning the lamb shanks once. Serve with mashed parsnip or celeriac and garnish with extra orange rind.

Roasted rack of lamb with ratatouille beans

This is smart entertaining without any hassle. Put the lamb on to roast when your friends arrive, then sit back and relax while it cooks. The garlicky Mediterranean vegetables, beans and meat juices combine to make a delicious and colourful accompaniment.

400 g (13 oz) can flageolet beans, rinsed
   and drained
2 racks of lamb, with 6 or 7 chops each
1 red pepper, cored, deseeded and diced
1 orange pepper, cored, deseeded and diced
2 small courgettes, diced
1 red onion, quartered
300 g (10 oz) cherry tomatoes, halved
3–4 garlic cloves, finely chopped
2 teaspoons ready-made pesto
2 tablespoons olive oil
salt and pepper

Put the beans in the centre of a roasting tin, season then lay the racks of lamb on top so that the fat is uppermost. Scatter the peppers, courgettes, onion, tomatoes and garlic around the lamb and season the dish with salt and pepper.

Spread pesto over the fat on each rack of lamb, then drizzle the oil over the meat and vegetables. Cook in a preheated oven, 200°C (400°F), Gas Mark 6, for 20 minutes for rare, 25 minutes for medium or 30 minutes for well done.

Cut the lamb into cutlets between the bones. Divide the beans and vegetables between 4 plates, and arrange the lamb cutlets on top.

Sizzling turkey and chorizo with beans

A few humble ingredients are transformed into a sensational feast in this Mediterranean-style supper dish. It tastes equally good eaten in the garden on a warm summer evening, or when you're curled up on the sofa on a cold winter night.

200 g (7 oz) frozen broad beans

200 g (7 oz) frozen whole green beans

3 tablespoons olive oil

375 g (12 oz) skinless, boneless turkey breast, cut into thin strips

2 onions, sliced

150 g (5 oz) chorizo, diced

2 tablespoons white wine vinegar

salt and pepper

handful of flat leaf parsley, to garnish

Cook the frozen beans in a saucepan of lightly salted boiling water for 3 minutes, or until tender.

Meanwhile, heat 2 tablespoons of the oil in a large frying pan, add the turkey and cook over a high heat until the underside is browned. Turn the turkey strips over and add the onions and chorizo with the remaining oil.

Fry for 8–10 minutes until the turkey and onions are browned and the turkey is cooked through. Stir in the drained beans, vinegar, salt and pepper, and cook for 1 minute. Serve garnished with torn parsley.

Sesame beef and noodles

Stir-fried beef has never tasted so good as here, flavoured with toasted sesame seeds and Thai curry paste. The addition of wilted pak choi, bean sprouts, shiitake mushrooms and rice noodles means it's not only delicious it's healthy too!

100 g (3½ oz) fine dried rice noodles

1–2 tablespoons sunflower oil

625 g (1¼ lb) sirloin steak, very thinly sliced

10 shiitake mushrooms, sliced

2 tablespoons sesame seeds

3 tablespoons soy sauce

4 teaspoons Thai red curry paste

1 bunch of red spring onions, cut into thin strips

175 g (6 oz) pak choi, sliced

250 g (8 oz) bean sprouts

1 tablespoon Thai fish sauce

Put the noodles into a bowl, cover with boiling water and leave to soak for 4 minutes, or according to packet instructions. Drain well.

Heat 1 tablespoon of the oil in a wok or large frying pan, add the beef and mushrooms and fry over a high heat for 1 minute. Add the sesame seeds and cook for 1 minute until lightly browned.

Add the soy sauce and curry paste and cook for 1 minute. Add the remaining vegetables and extra oil, if necessary, and stir-fry for 2 minutes. Add the noodles and fish sauce and warm through, then spoon into warmed serving bowls and serve immediately.

Seared lamb noisettes with leek and caper confetti

A bed of buttery fried leeks flavoured with capers, pink peppercorns and chopped mint, then topped with lamb chops grilled with redcurrant jelly, makes an elegant meal for a special occasion.

8 loin lamb chops
3 tablespoons redcurrant jelly
1 tablespoon olive oil
25 g (1 oz) butter
2 leeks, thinly sliced
1 tablespoon capers, drained and rinsed
small handful rosemary or mint leaves,
    plus extra to garnish
2 teaspoons pink peppercorns in brine,
    drained
salt and pepper

Roll up the lamb chops tightly and secure each with two cocktail sticks. Put the chops on a foil-lined grill pan, dot with the redcurrant jelly and season with salt and pepper. Cook under a preheated hot grill for 5 minutes, turn over, spoon the redcurrant jelly juices over the lamb and cook for 5 minutes more.

Meanwhile, heat the oil and butter in a frying pan, add the leeks, capers, snipped herbs and peppercorns and stir-fry for 5 minutes until softened and just beginning to brown. Spoon on to individual plates.

Arrange the lamb on top of the leeks, remove the cocktail sticks and sprinkle with extra snipped herbs.

One-pot barbecue bake

Ideal for a family meal, you can simply put all the ingredients in a roasting tin, brush with a barbecue glaze and leave it to cook. A refreshing green salad makes a great accompaniment.

4 chicken thighs
4 chicken drumsticks
4 large sausages
1 kg (2 lb) new potatoes
1 red pepper, cored, deseeded
    and cut into 8
2 onions, cut into 8
4 or 5 bay leaves
green salad, to serve

GLAZE

2 tablespoons sunflower oil
2 tablespoons tomato ketchup
2 tablespoons light muscovado
    sugar
2 tablespoons wine vinegar
1 tablespoon Worcestershire sauce
salt and pepper

Slash each chicken piece 2 or 3 times with a knife, then place in a roasting tin. Pinch the centre of each sausage, twist then cut in half. Put them into the tin with the potatoes, pepper and onions, and tuck the bay leaves under the chicken.

Mix the glaze ingredients together and season with salt and pepper. Brush over the ingredients in the tin then cook in a preheated oven, 190°C (375°F), Gas Mark 5, for 50–60 minutes, basting with the juices once during cooking and turning the potatoes, as needed, until browned.

Pierce the potatoes and chicken with a small knife to check that they are tender and make sure that the meat juices run clear. Spoon on to plates and serve with salad.

Chicken skewers with pistachio salad

Cajun-spiced chicken skewers taste great cooked over the barbecue in summer, or under the grill in winter. Served with a hearty salad of crisp leaves, avocado and pistachio nuts, they make a surprisingly substantial meal. You can also make the skewers using lamb or beef if you prefer.

4 skinless, boneless chicken breasts,
    about 150 g (5 oz) each
5 tablespoons olive oil
large pinch of Cajun spice mix
1 large ripe avocado, peeled, stoned
    and diced
2 tablespoons lime juice
40 g (1½ oz) pistachio nuts,
    roughly chopped
small handful of fresh coriander leaves
125 g (4 oz) mixed salad leaves
salt and pepper

Cut the chicken breasts into cubes, thread these on to 8 skewers and arrange on a rack over a foil-lined grill pan. Drizzle with a little of the oil and sprinkle with the Cajun spice mix. Season with salt and pepper and cook under a preheated hot grill for 10 minutes, turning once or twice, until browned and cooked through.

Meanwhile, put the avocado into a bowl and toss with the lime juice. Add the remaining olive oil and season with salt and pepper. Add the pistachios to the bowl with the salad leaves and torn coriander leaves. Toss together gently, then spoon on to plates and top with the cooked chicken skewers.

Beef and chickpea tagine

Mince makes a great standby, and here it is transformed with Middle Eastern spices to create a mellow, well-rounded, flavourful stew. Serve with warmed pitta breads.

1 tablespoon olive oil
1 onion, finely chopped
500 g (1 lb) extra lean minced beef
2 carrots, diced
200 g (7 oz) swede, diced
2 garlic cloves, crushed
400 g (13 oz) can chickpeas, rinsed and drained
1 dried red chilli
1 teaspoon turmeric
½ teaspoon ground cinnamon
½ teaspoon ground allspice
400 g (13 oz) can chopped tomatoes
450 ml (¾ pint) chicken stock
125 g (4 oz) frozen peas, cooked
small bunch of mint leaves, snipped
salt and pepper
warmed pitta breads, to serve

Heat the oil in a heatproof casserole dish, add the onion and mince and fry, stirring occasionally, until browned. Stir the carrots, swede and garlic into the pan along with the chickpeas. Mix in the dried chilli and ground spices and cook for 1 minute.

Add the tomatoes, stock, salt and pepper, then bring to the boil, stirring. Cover and cook in a preheated oven, 180°C (350°F), Gas Mark 4, for 1½ hours. Stir then top with the cooked peas and snipped mint leaves and serve in bowls with warmed pitta breads.

Pork Dijonnaise

Tender pork fillet cooked with cider, wholegrain French mustard and a dash of cream makes a quick and easy bistro-style supper. Serve with a mixture of white and wild rice.

1 tablespoon olive oil
15 g (½ oz) butter
500 g (1 lb) pork fillet, thinly sliced
1 onion, thinly sliced
2 garlic cloves, crushed
300 ml (½ pint) dry cider
2 teaspoons wholegrain mustard
3 tablespoons double cream
salt and pepper
chopped chives, to garnish
cooked white and wild rice, to serve

Heat the oil and butter in a large frying pan, add the pork, onion and garlic and fry over a high heat for 4–5 minutes, stirring, until the pork is browned on both sides.

Add the cider and mustard, season with salt and pepper and boil rapidly for 3–4 minutes until the cider has reduced slightly. Lower the heat and stir in the cream. Sprinkle with the chopped chives and serve with white and wild rice.

Lamb's liver with cranberries and bacon

Lamb's liver takes only the briefest time to cook and has a wonderful flavour and succulent texture. Here it is complemented with a rich sauce made with sweet cranberries, caramelized onions, crispy bacon and a dash of red wine vinegar.

2 tablespoons olive oil

2 onions, thinly sliced

150 g (5 oz) smoked back bacon, diced

25 g (1 oz) butter

625 g (1¼ lb) sliced lamb's liver

2 tablespoons cranberry sauce

2 tablespoons red wine vinegar

75 g (3 oz) frozen cranberries

2 tablespoons water

salt and pepper

mashed potatoes, to serve

Heat the oil in a large frying pan, add the onions and bacon and fry over a medium heat for 10 minutes, stirring occasionally, until they are a deep golden brown. Remove from the pan and set aside.

Melt the butter in the pan and add the liver slices. Fry for 3 minutes over a high heat, turning once or twice, until browned on the outside and just pink in the centre. Add the cranberry sauce, vinegar, cranberries and measured water.

Season with salt and pepper and cook for 2 minutes, stirring until the cranberry sauce has melted and the cranberries are soft and heated through. Stir in the fried onions and bacon. Serve with mashed potatoes.

Warm turkey foccacia

These jumbo open sandwiches are topped with hot strips of turkey, sun-dried tomatoes, basil and rocket. The olive tapenade made from crushed black olives, gives a real boost to the flavour.

1 tablespoon olive oil

250 g (8 oz) skinless, boneless turkey fillet,
   cut into thin strips

1 onion, thinly sliced

2 foccacia loaves, thickly sliced

2 tablespoons black olive tapenade

100 g (3½ oz) sun-dried tomatoes in oil,
   drained and sliced

4 tomatoes, roughly chopped

handful of basil leaves (optional)

salt and pepper

rocket leaves, to garnish

Heat the oil in a large frying pan, add the turkey and onion and fry for 5 minutes, stirring until browned.

Lightly toast the foccacia slices on both sides. Spread thinly with olive tapenade and drizzle with a little oil from the jar of sun-dried tomatoes.

Add the fresh and sun-dried tomatoes to the turkey, with the basil leaves, if using, and season with salt and pepper. Cook for 3 minutes, then spoon on to the toasted foccacia and top with rocket leaves. Serve immediately.

Chicken with 20 cloves of garlic

Don't be put off by the quantity of garlic used in this recipe, which is also known as *Le poulet sauté Dauphinois*. Slow cooking lessens the intensity of its flavour and gives a deliciously sweet, mellow result. Peel off the papery garlic skins to reveal the soft, sweet flesh beneath.

2 tablespoons plain flour
4 chicken leg quarters
2 tablespoons olive oil
1 onion, chopped
75 g (3 oz) pancetta, diced
200 ml (7 fl oz) dry white wine
300 ml (½ pint) chicken stock
1½ teaspoons Dijon mustard
20 garlic cloves, unpeeled

1 dried bouquet garni
salt and pepper
fresh parsley, rosemary and
    thyme, to garnish
boiled new potatoes, to serve

Put the flour into a plastic bag and season generously with salt and pepper. Add 2 chicken quarters and shake to cover lightly. Repeat with the remaining 2 quarters.

Heat half the oil in a large frying pan, add half the chicken and fry until golden brown on both sides. Lift out of the pan and transfer to a heatproof casserole dish. Heat the remaining oil and fry the rest of the chicken joints in the same way.

Add the onion and pancetta to the pan and fry until lightly browned. Stir in any remaining flour from the plastic bag, then add the wine, stock, mustard, garlic and bouquet garni. Bring to the boil.

Pour the mixture over the chicken, cover and cook in a preheated oven, 180°C (350°F), Gas Mark 4, for 1¼ hours until the chicken is tender. Spoon on to plates, garnish with snipped parsley, rosemary and thyme and serve with new potatoes.

Turkey and courgette eggah

Of Arab origin, an eggah is rather like an Italian frittata or Spanish tortilla and can be cooked in a frying pan or in the oven. Serve warm or cold as a main meal, with salads, chutneys and warmed bread, or cut into tiny squares as an appetizer.

1 tablespoon olive oil, plus extra for greasing

1 onion, chopped

200 g (7 oz) skinless, boneless turkey breast, diced

175 g (6 oz) courgettes, halved lengthways
  and sliced

4 tablespoons roughly chopped mint leaves

6 eggs, beaten

salt and pepper

tomato salad, to serve

Heat the oil in a frying pan, add the onion and fry for 2–3 minutes. Add the turkey and fry over a high heat until just beginning to brown. Add the courgettes and fry them for 1–2 minutes. Tip the mixture into a greased shallow ovenproof dish.

Mix the mint with the beaten egg and season with salt and pepper. Pour over the turkey mixture and cook in a preheated oven, 180°C (350°F), Gas Mark 4, for about 25 minutes until set and golden. Leave to stand for a minute or so, then cut into pieces and serve with a tomato salad.

Venison sausages with spicy bean and vegetable sauce

After a hard day at work, this hearty dish should soon restore flagging energy levels. The spicy sauce, chunky vegetables and meaty venison sausages are sure to give you the boost you need. Serve in bowls with warmed crusty bread.

8 venison sausages
1 tablespoon sunflower oil
1 onion, chopped
1 red pepper, cored, deseeded and diced
1 courgette, diced
2 flat cap mushrooms, sliced
400 g (13 oz) can red kidney beans, rinsed
    and drained
400 g (13 oz) can chopped tomatoes
1 teaspoon chopped red chilli
1 teaspoon wholegrain mustard
2 teaspoons brown sugar
salt and pepper
crusty bread, to serve

Cook the sausages under a preheated hot grill for 10–12 minutes until browned and cooked through. Meanwhile, heat the oil in a large frying pan, add the onion and cook for 3 minutes.

Add the pepper, courgette and mushrooms and cook for 3 minutes. Stir in the remaining ingredients, bring to the boil, cover and simmer for 5 minutes until the sauce is thick.

Spoon the beans into bowls and serve with the sausages and crusty bread.

Desserts

Caramelized clementines
with star anise

A great festive dessert, this fruit salad is ideal when feeding lots of people – simply multiply the quantities. A few sprigs of fresh rosemary or a couple of bay leaves can be used in place of the star anise to flavour the syrup.

250 g (8 oz) granulated sugar
250 ml (8 fl oz) cold water
6 tablespoons boiling water
8 clementines, peeled
3 whole star anise
cream or crème fraîche, to serve

Put the sugar and cold water into a small saucepan and heat gently, without stirring, until the sugar has completely dissolved. Increase the heat and boil for about 10 minutes until just turning pale golden.

Don't be tempted to stir the mixture or the sugar will harden – tilt the pan to mix the sugar, if needed. Take the pan off the heat and add the boiling water, a tablespoon at a time, standing well back after each addition as it will spit. Tilt the pan to mix, heating gently if needed.

Put the clementines into a heatproof bowl with the star anise, then pour over the hot syrup and leave to cool for 3–4 hours. Stir the clementines and transfer to a serving dish. Serve with cream or crème fraîche.

Quick summer puddings with vodka

Forget about overnight chilling – this modern, adults-only summer pudding is made by layering circles of bread with a bag of frozen berries mixed with a little caster sugar and a splash of vodka. Use a microwave to defrost the fruits, or leave them at room temperature for an hour.

375 g (12 oz) frozen mixed berries, thawed
3 tablespoons vodka
40 g (1½ oz) caster sugar
8 slices of white bread
vanilla ice cream, to serve

Tip the fruit into a sieve set over a bowl. When the juice has run out, transfer the fruit to a second bowl and mix in the vodka and the sugar.

Stamp out 7.5-cm (3-inch) circles from the bread, using a fluted pastry cutter. Dip both sides of 4 pieces of bread into the berry juice then place them in individual shallow glass serving dishes.

Spoon half the fruit over the bread circles, then cover with the remaining bread dipped into the juice. Top with the remaining fruit and juices from the bowl. Serve with vanilla ice cream.

Honeyed panna cotta with nectarines

This popular Italian-style dessert is made with a decadent mix of double cream, mascarpone cheese and wild-flower honey for a deliciously creamy, softly set dessert.

3 tablespoons water

3 teaspoons or 1 sachet of powdered gelatine

300 ml (½ pint) double cream

150 ml (¼ pint) semi-skimmed milk

4 tablespoons thick-set wild-flower honey

125 g (4 oz) mascarpone cheese

2 nectarines, stoned, halved and sliced

125 g (4 oz) raspberries

mint leaves, to decorate

Put the measured water into a small bowl, sprinkle the gelatine over the top, making sure that all the powder has been absorbed. Set aside for 3–4 minutes. Meanwhile, put the cream, milk and honey into a saucepan and heat gently until the honey has dissolved.

Bring the cream just to the boil, then take it off the heat and add the gelatine, then stir occasionally until the soaked gelatine has completely dissolved. Add the mascarpone and whisk until smooth.

Pour the mixture into 4 200-ml (7-fl oz) moulds. Cool, then chill for 4–5 hours or until set. To turn out, dip each mould into a bowl of hot water. After 10 seconds, loosen the edges of the desserts, then invert the moulds on to small plates. Holding the mould and plate, jerk to release, then remove the mould. Decorate with mint leaves, and serve with the nectarines and raspberries.

Strawberry and lavender crush

Capture the essence of summer with this delicately flavoured, light strawberry and meringue dessert that is, quite literally, made in minutes. If you don't have fresh lavender at home, buy a small pot from a garden centre or use a few dried flowers instead.

400 g (13 oz) strawberries
2 tablespoons icing sugar, plus extra
   to decorate
4–5 lavender flowers, plus extra
   to decorate
400 g (13 oz) Greek yogurt
4 ready-made meringue nests

Reserving 4 small strawberries for decoration, hull and mash the remainder with the icing sugar using a fork or in a food processor. Pull off the lavender flowers from the stems and crumble them into the strawberries to taste.

Put the yogurt in a bowl, crumble in the meringues then lightly mix together. Add the strawberry mixture, fold together with a spoon until marbled, then spoon into glasses.

Cut the reserved strawberries in half, then decorate the desserts with the strawberry halves and lavender flowers. Lightly dust with icing sugar and serve immediately.

Iced pineapple and ginger torte

This creamy, iced meringue gâteau, speckled with pineapple, ginger and tangy lime rind, slices beautifully and is perfect for serving after a hot curry or chilli. If you like, make it a day or more in advance, but allow it to defrost for 10–15 minutes before serving for easy slicing.

150 ml (¼ pint) double cream

200 g (7 oz) sweetened condensed milk

finely grated rind and juice of 1 lime

2 tablespoons candied ginger, chopped

250 g (8 oz) canned pineapple chunks, drained and finely chopped

2 ready-made meringue nests, crumbled

1 kiwi fruit, sliced, to decorate

Whip the cream until softly peaking then fold in the condensed milk, lime rind and juice and ginger. Stir the pineapple and meringues into the cream mixture, then pour into a 500 g (1 lb) loaf tin lined with clingfilm.

Level the surface and freeze for 4–5 hours until firm. Loosen the edges, then turn out on to a serving plate. Remove the clingfilm, decorate the top with sliced kiwi fruit, and cut into slices to serve.

Exotic fruit salad

A refreshing blend of green melon, perfumed papaya and mango, tossed with eye-catching kiwi slices and a tangy lime syrup, makes the perfect dessert for an Asian-style meal. Either make it just before you eat, or prepare the fruits earlier in the day and keep chilled until ready to serve.

2 tablespoons caster sugar

4 tablespoons boiling water

finely grated rind and juice of 1 lime

1 Galia melon, peeled, deseeded and cut into chunks

1 papaya, peeled, deseeded and cut into chunks

2 kiwi fruits, peeled, halved and sliced

1 ripe mango, peeled, stoned and diced

1 pomegranate (optional)

Put the sugar into a small bowl with the measured boiling water and stir until dissolved. Mix in the lime rind and juice.

Put all the prepared fruits into a glass serving dish and add the syrup. Toss together gently. Cut the pomegranate in half, if using, and pop out the seeds. Sprinkle over the fruit salad and chill until you are ready to serve it.

Chocolate espresso mousses

For a decadent end to a meal, make these rich, dark mousses in tiny coffee cups and serve topped with spoonfuls of extra-thick double cream that can be spooned straight from the tub. Decorate with a sprinkling of cocoa or drinking chocolate powder or make some chocolate curls.

1 tablespoon ground espresso coffee
100 ml (3½ fl oz) boiling water
100 g (3½ oz) plain dark chocolate, broken
   into pieces
knob of butter
pinch of ground cinnamon
2 small eggs, separated
15 g (½ oz) caster sugar
extra-thick double cream, to decorate

Put the coffee into a cafetiére, pour the measured boiling water on top and leave to brew for a few minutes. Melt the chocolate with the butter and cinnamon in a heatproof bowl placed over a saucepan of gently simmering water.

Stir the egg yolks into the chocolate, one at a time. Strain the coffee, then gradually stir it into the chocolate mixture.

Take off the heat, whisk the egg whites until they form soft peaks, then gradually whisk in the sugar. Fold a large spoonful into the chocolate mixture to loosen it, then add the remainder and fold in gently with a large metal spoon.

Pour the mousse into small coffee cups and chill for 4 hours until set. Top with spoonfuls of extra-thick cream and decorate with whatever version of chocolate you prefer.

Chocolate bread and butter pudding

Bread and butter pudding is one of those timeless desserts that is adored by young and old alike. For an extra-indulgent treat, this version is made with a rich chocolate sauce and a sweet vanilla custard. If you prefer, you can use fruit bread or croissants instead of the French bread.

150 g (5 oz) plain dark chocolate, broken
   into pieces
250 g (8 oz) French bread, thinly sliced
50 g (2 oz) butter, at room temperature
3 eggs
50 g (2 oz) caster sugar
1 teaspoon vanilla essence
large pinch of ground cinnamon
450 ml (¾ pint) full-fat milk
single cream, to serve

Melt the chocolate in a heatproof bowl placed over a saucepan of gently simmering water. Spread the bread with some of the butter, then add the remainder of the butter to the chocolate.

Cover the bottom of a greased 1.5 litre (2½ pint) ovenproof dish with a layer of bread and butter. Stir the chocolate, then spoon a little over the bread. Continue layering bread and chocolate until you reach the top of the dish.

Whisk the eggs, sugar, vanilla, cinnamon and milk together, then pour over the bread and butter. Cover loosely with buttered foil and leave to stand for 15 minutes. Cook in a preheated oven, 180°C (350°F), Gas Mark 4, for 35 minutes or until the custard has set, removing the foil for the last 5 minutes to brown the top. Serve with cream.

Sultana and ginger rice pudding

This fruity, zesty, spicy rice pudding offers a modern twist to the classic nursery pudding. To make a rather adult, orange-flavoured version, soak the sultanas in a tablespoon or two of Grand Marnier or Cointreau before cooking, and use orange rind in place of the lemon rind.

65 g (2½ oz) pudding rice
2 tablespoons caster sugar
2 tablespoons sultanas
1 tablespoon ready-chopped candied ginger
finely grated rind of ½ lemon
600 ml (1 pint) full-fat milk
25 g (½ oz) butter
grated nutmeg

Put the rice, sugar, sultanas, ginger and lemon rind into a 1.2 litre (2 pint) shallow ovenproof dish. Pour the cold milk over the top and mix the ingredients together.

Cut the butter into tiny pieces and dot over the top of the milk. Sprinkle with a little nutmeg and cook in a preheated oven, 150°C (300°F), Gas Mark 2, for 2 hours until the top is golden brown, the rice tender and the milk thick and creamy. Serve warm.

Rhubarb, pear and marzipan crumble

Quick and easy to put together, this richly flavoured crumble makes an ideal midweek pudding or a fabulous treat after a Sunday roast. The crumble mix can be made in bulk and stored in a plastic bag in the freezer, ready for an instant dessert whenever the mood takes you.

400 g (13 oz) trimmed rhubarb, thinly sliced

1 ripe pear, peeled, cored and sliced

100 g (3½ oz) caster sugar

125 g (4 oz) plain flour

50 g (2 oz) butter, cut into pieces

125 g (4 oz) marzipan, coarsely grated

flaked almonds, for sprinkling

custard, to serve

Put the rhubarb and pear into a 1.2 litre (2 pint) ovenproof pie dish with half the sugar.

Put the rest of the sugar into a food processor, add the flour and butter and process until the mixture resembles fine breadcrumbs. Alternatively, put the ingredients into a mixing bowl and rub in the butter with your fingertips. Stir in the grated marzipan.

Spoon over the fruit and sprinkle with a few flaked almonds. Cook in a preheated oven, 180°C (350°F), Gas Mark 4, for 35–40 minutes until golden brown, checking after 15–20 minutes and covering with foil if necessary. Serve immediately with custard.

Soufflé jam omelette

This light, fluffy soufflé can be made in minutes – first cooked in a frying pan and then flashed under a hot grill to brown the top. The raspberry jam, raspberries and blueberries make for a luxurious dessert. Frozen berries make a great standby and can be defrosted in the microwave in just a few minutes if you haven't had a chance to buy fresh.

6 eggs, separated
2 teaspoons vanilla essence
4 tablespoons icing sugar
40 g (1½ oz) butter
4 tablespoons raspberry jam
100 g (3½ oz) raspberries
100 g (3½ oz) blueberries
single cream, to serve

Whisk the egg whites in a large bowl until they form soft peaks. Put the yolks, vanilla and 1 tablespoon of the sugar in a separate bowl and use the same whisk to beat them together. Fold a spoonful of the egg whites into the yolks to loosen the mixture then add the remainder and fold them in gently with a large metal spoon.

Heat half the butter in a 20 cm (8 inch) frying pan. Pour in half the egg mixture and cook for 3–4 minutes until the underside is golden. Quickly flash the omelette under a preheated hot grill for 1–2 minutes to brown the top. Slide into a shallow dish and quickly make a second omelette in the same way with the remaining ingredients.

Dot the omelettes with the jam and fruit, then fold in half to enclose the filling. Dust the tops with the remaining icing sugar, cut in half and serve immediately with cream.

Striped berry syllabubs

Light and refreshing, this quick summer dessert is perfect for last-minute entertaining. You can use all kinds of soft fruits in place of the strawberries if you prefer. Why not try crumbled raspberries or puréed mango instead?

300 ml (½ pint) double cream
5 tablespoons caster sugar
finely grated rind of 1 lemon
150 ml (¼ pint) dry cider
200 g (7 oz) strawberries, hulled
200 g (7 oz) raspberries, defrosted
   if frozen

Pour the cream into a bowl, add 3 tablespoons of the sugar and the lemon rind and whisk until the cream forms soft peaks. Gradually whisk in the cider then set aside.

Reserve 4 of the smallest strawberries for decoration, then mash the remainder with the raspberries and the remaining sugar.

Spoon one-third of the cream mixture into 4 wine glasses. Use half the mashed berries to make a thin layer over the cream, then repeat the layers finishing with a layer of cream. Decorate each glass with a strawberry and chill until required.

American blueberry and lemon pancakes

Thick American pancakes make a great simple dessert, but they're also perfect for a weekend breakfast or brunch. If you can't find fresh blueberries, you can use sultanas or even canned cherries instead.

125 g (4 oz) self-raising flour
finely grated rind of ½ lemon
1 teaspoon baking powder
1 tablespoon caster sugar
1 egg
1 tablespoon lemon juice
150 ml (¼ pint) semi-skimmed milk
125 g (4 oz) blueberries, plus extra to decorate
oil, for frying

TO SERVE
maple syrup
ice cream

Put the flour, lemon rind, baking powder and sugar into a bowl. Add the egg and lemon juice then gradually whisk in the milk until you have a smooth, thick batter. Stir in the blueberries.

Heat a griddle or large frying pan then rub it with a piece of kitchen paper drizzled with a little oil. Drop spoonfuls of the mixture, well spaced apart, on the griddle or pan and cook for 2–3 minutes until bubbles form on the surface and the underside is golden brown.

Turn the pancakes over and cook the second side. Wrap in a tea cloth and keep hot while you cook the remaining mixture in the same way. Stack on four plates and drizzle with maple syrup and decorate with a few extra blueberries. Serve with ice cream.

Apple fritters with blackberry sauce

Dainty slices of apple, veiled in a light, sweet batter, then deep-fried until crisp and golden, taste divine served with warmed blackberries. For an extra treat, serve with big scoops of vanilla ice cream. Thick slices of banana can be used in place of the apples if you prefer.

2 eggs
125 g (4 oz) plain flour
4 tablespoons caster sugar
150 ml (¼ pint) milk
sunflower oil, for deep frying
4 dessert apples, cored and thickly sliced
150 g (5 oz) frozen blackberries
2 tablespoons water
sifted icing sugar, for dusting

Separate one egg and put the white into one bowl and the yolk and the whole egg into a second bowl. Add the flour and half the sugar to the second bowl. Whisk the egg white until softly peaking, then use the same whisk to beat the flour mixture until smooth, gradually whisking in the milk. Fold in the egg white.

Pour the oil into a saucepan until it comes one-third of the way up, then heat to 190°C (375°F), or until a drop of batter bubbles instantly when added. Add a few apple slices to the batter and turn gently to coat. Lift out one slice at a time and lower carefully into the oil. Cook in batches for 2–3 minutes, turning until evenly golden. Lift out with a slotted spoon and drain on kitchen paper.

Meanwhile, put the blackberries, remaining sugar and measured water into a small saucepan and heat for 2–3 minutes until hot. Arrange the fritters on serving plates, spoon the blackberry sauce around and dust with a little sifted icing sugar.

Baked peaches with amaretti and raspberries

A quick, yet utterly irresistible dessert that is just as good served after a simple supper or an elegant dinner party. Amaretto accentuates the delicious almond flavour of the dessert, but it is just as good made with Grand Marnier, Cointreau or sherry.

4 ripe peaches or nectarines, halved and stoned
40 g (1½ oz) amaretti biscuits, crumbled
150 g (5 oz) fresh or frozen raspberries
2 tablespoons redcurrant jelly
2 tablespoons Amaretto liqueur
2 tablespoons water
vanilla ice cream, to serve

Arrange the peaches or nectarines, cut sides up, in a shallow ovenproof dish. Crumble the biscuits into a bowl then mix in a few of the raspberries, the redcurrant jelly and the liqueur and mix together gently.

Spoon the biscuit mixture on top of the peaches, then sprinkle the remaining raspberries in the dish. Pour the measured water into the dish, then cook, uncovered, in a preheated oven, 180°C (350°F), Gas Mark 4, for 15 minutes until hot. Serve with vanilla ice cream.

Cherry and cinnamon zabaglione

A classic Italian dessert, this light bubbly custard is flavoured with sherry and a hint of cinnamon and is whisked over hot water for maximum volume. It makes the perfect partner for warmed cherries and a great standby for unexpected guests. Measure out the ingredients before you sit down to your main course so that you can whip up the dessert in moments.

4 egg yolks
125 g (4 oz) caster sugar
150 ml (¼ pint) cream sherry
large pinch of ground cinnamon
425 g (14 oz) can black cherries
   in syrup
2 amaretti biscuits, crumbled,
   to decorate

Pour 5 cm (2 inches) of water into a medium saucepan and bring to the boil. Cover with a large mixing bowl, making sure that the water does not touch the base of the bowl. Reduce the heat so that the water is simmering, then add the egg yolks, sugar, sherry and cinnamon to the bowl. Whisk for 5–8 minutes until very thick and foamy and the custard leaves a trail when the whisk is lifted above the mixture.

Drain off some of the cherry syrup and then tip the cherries and just a little of the syrup into a small saucepan. Warm through, then spoon into 4 glasses. Pour the warm zabaglione over the top and decorate with crumbled amaretti biscuits. Serve immediately.

Lemon posset with frosted grapes

Rather like a rich, set lemon custard, this wonderfully simple dessert is served in pretty glass dishes. It tastes delicious with sugar-coated frosted grapes, but could also be served with sliced strawberries or a mixed summer berry compote.

300 ml (½ pint) double cream
75 g (3 oz) caster sugar
finely grated rind of ½ lemon
4 tablespoons lemon juice

FROSTED GRAPES

1 egg white or reconstituted egg white
25 g (1 oz) caster sugar
150 g (5 oz) white seedless grapes

Pour the cream into a small saucepan, add the sugar and lemon rind and heat gently until the sugar has dissolved. Simmer over a medium heat for 2–3 minutes until the edges of the cream are bubbling gently. Take off the heat and stir in the lemon juice then pour into 4 small glass dishes.

Lightly whisk the egg white in a bowl until frothy and put the sugar into a second bowl. Snip the grapes into tiny bunches, each with 3 or 4 grapes. Dip them first into the egg white then into the sugar and lay them on a serving plate. Chill the desserts and the grapes for 4 hours, or until the lemon mixture has set. Arrange the grapes on top of the desserts to serve.

Gooseberry and elderflower fool

A light and tangy fool with just a hint of elderflower makes a creamy, indulgent dessert. It's great when you want a no-fuss end to a meal because it can be made in advance and left to chill until you are ready to serve it. Elderflower cordial can be found in most supermarkets, but if you don't have any, you can simply use water instead.

500 g (1 lb) frozen gooseberries, plus extra to decorate

3 tablespoons undiluted elderflower cordial

100 g (3½ oz) caster sugar, plus extra to decorate

125 g (4 oz) mascarpone cheese

150 g (5 oz) ready-made low-fat custard

biscuits, to serve

Put the frozen gooseberries into a saucepan with the cordial and sugar and cook, uncovered, for 5 minutes, stirring until softened. Transfer to a blender or food processor and blend until smooth.

Add the mascarpone and custard and blend briefly until mixed. Press the mixture through a sieve, if you like, then pour it into individual serving dishes.

Chill for several hours, then decorate the top with a few extra defrosted gooseberries rolled in a little extra sugar. Serve with dainty, crisp biscuits.

Cranberry and orange sponge puddings

Delightfully light and fluffy, these zesty orange sponges, topped with tangy cranberries and a luscious orange sauce, make a surprisingly light winter pudding. Put them on to cook just before you sit down to your main course and they will be ready by the time you clear the plates.

finely grated rind and juice of 1 orange
150 g (5 oz) frozen cranberries
100 g (3½ oz) caster sugar
2 tablespoons raspberry jam
100 g (3½ oz) soft margarine
100 g (3½ oz) self-raising flour
2 eggs
custard, to serve

Put the orange juice into a saucepan with the frozen cranberries and 1 tablespoon of sugar and cook over a moderate heat for 5 minutes until the cranberries are just softened. Use a slotted spoon to drain and spoon half the cranberries into 4 individual 200 ml (7 fl oz) metal pudding moulds.

Add the jam to the remaining cranberries and cook for 1 minute until melted. Set aside.

Put the remaining sugar, the margarine, flour, eggs and orange rind into a bowl or food processor and beat until smooth. Spoon the sponge mixture into the moulds and level the surface. Cover loosely with pieces of oiled foil.

Cook the puddings in the top of a steamer or in a preheated oven, 180°C (350°F), Gas Mark 4, for 25 minutes until well risen. Loosen the edges with a round-bladed knife and turn out on to serving plates. Top with the remaining cranberries and serve with custard.

Florentine stackers

Transform shop-bought Florentines into a sophisticated dessert by sandwiching them with mashed bananas and honey-flavoured fromage frais, and serving them with a fresh strawberry coulis. Round Langue de chat or Tuille biscuits could be used instead of the Florentines.

1 ripe banana, mashed
125 g (4 oz) fromage frais
1 tablespoon clear honey
8 Florentine biscuits
250 g (8 oz) strawberries
mint leaves, to decorate

Mix the banana in a bowl with the fromage frais and honey. Use this mixture to sandwich the Florentine biscuits together in pairs.

Purée the strawberries in a blender or food processor, then sieve the mixture and discard the seeds.

Arrange the biscuits on individual plates and spoon the sauce around them. Decorate with mint leaves and serve immediately.

Orange palmiers with plums

These crisp, delicate pastries look very professional, but they can be made in minutes, using a pack of ready-rolled puff pastry. Simply unravel, sprinkle with sugar and grated orange rind, roll up and slice. Sandwich baked pastries with a warm plum compote or vary the fruit to suit the season – rhubarb, greengages and raspberries also work well.

1 sheet of ready-rolled frozen puff pastry, about 25 cm (10 inches) square, thawed
beaten egg, for brushing
3 tablespoons light muscovado sugar
finely grated rind of $\frac{1}{2}$ orange
6 tablespoons orange juice

50 g (2 oz) caster sugar
400 g (13 oz) plums, stoned and sliced
sifted icing sugar, to decorate
crème fraîche, to serve

Brush the pastry with beaten egg, then sprinkle with the muscovado sugar and orange rind. Roll one edge of the pastry until it reaches the middle. Do the same from the opposite edge until both rolls meet.

Brush with more beaten egg, then cut into 8 thick slices. Arrange, cut slices uppermost, on a lightly oiled baking sheet. Bake in a preheated oven, 200°C (400°F), Gas Mark 6, for 10 minutes until well risen and golden.

Meanwhile, put the orange juice and sugar into a saucepan. Add the plums and cook uncovered for 5 minutes.

Sandwich the palmiers in pairs with the plums, dust with sifted icing sugar and serve with crème fraîche.

Peach strudel fingers

Filo pastry is perfect for making a simple, speedy strudel. Just unfold and separate the sheets, then brush them with butter and roll them around the lightly spiced peach and almond mixture. The strudel fingers are delicious eaten warm from the oven with a big spoonful of cream or ice cream.

3 ripe peaches, stoned and thinly sliced

2 tablespoons caster sugar, plus extra to decorate

2 tablespoons ground almonds

½ teaspoon ground cinnamon

2 tablespoons sultanas

6 sheets of filo pastry, 30 x 18 cm
   (12 x 7 inches) each

40 g (1½ oz) butter, melted

sifted icing sugar, to decorate

whipped cream or crème fraîche, to serve

Put the peaches into a bowl with the sugar, ground almonds, cinnamon and sultanas and toss gently together. Lay a sheet of pastry on a work surface, with the longest edge towards you and brush it with a little of the melted butter. Spoon a quarter of the peach mixture horizontally (or follow the longest edge) in a line down the centre, stopping about 5 cm (2 inches) in from either end.

Fold the short sides of the pastry over the filling. Fold one long side over the filling, then roll up to enclose the filling completely. Transfer the strudel to a baking sheet and repeat to make 3 more.

Cut the remaining pastry sheets in half. Brush the outside edges of the strudels with a little more butter then roll them up in the remaining sheets of pastry. Brush with the remaining butter. Cook in a preheated oven, 180°C (350°F), Gas Mark 4, for 10–13 minutes, until golden brown. Sprinkle with a little icing sugar and serve warm with whipped cream or crème fraîche.

Index

Acknowledgements

Executive Editor Nicky Hill

Senior Editor Rachel Lawrence

Executive Art Editor Geoff Fennell

Designer Janis Utton

Production Controller Manjit Sihra

Special Photography William Lingwood

Food Stylists Tonia George and Sara Lewis

Props Stylist Angela Swaffield